자르는선

KEYTERM
MASTER
MINIBOOK

KEY TERMS
IN ENGLISH LANGUAGE TEACHING
FOR PRE-SERVICE TEACHERS

www.pmg.co.kr

KB065353

교원임용시험 전공영어대비

KEYTERM MASTER

MINIBOOK

Song Eun Woo

동영상강의 박문각임용
www.pmg.co.kr

KEYTERM
MASTER
for EFL teachers

How to use
this book

챕터별 Key Terms를 Keyterm Minibook으로 제작하였습니다.

Keyterm Minibook을 어디서든지 휴대하여

간편하게 나의 학습 정도를 확인해보세요.

하루 한 번 Key Terms 복습을 목표로 하여 아직 학습이

부족한 단어는 꼭 Check 박스에 표시하세요.

그리고 《Keyterm Master》로 돌아가 해당 Term의

Definitions과 Key Phrase를 다시 확인하세요.

학습 내용을 보완하고 더 깊은 이해를 도모할 수 있습니다.

또한, Key Terms 마스터에 가까워지기 위해서는 최소 3번의 복습이

필요하다는 것을 기억하세요! 오늘도 즐겁게 공부합시다! 화이팅 :-)

Basic Concepts and Perspectives in SLA

(Principles & Models)

Check ✎

001 **Acquisition-learning hypothesis** ☐☐☐

002 **Acquisition** ☐☐☐

003 **Additive bilingualism** ☐☐☐

004 **Affective filter hypothesis** ☐☐☐

005 **Analyzed language** ☐☐☐

006 **Anomie** ☐☐☐

007 **Audiolingualism** ☐☐☐

008 **Automatic processes (=processing) / Automaticity** ☐☐☐

009 **Backsliding** ☐☐☐

010 **Behaviorism** ☐☐☐

011 **Bilingualism** ☐☐☐

012 **Coherence** ☐☐☐

013 **Cohesion** ☐☐☐

014 **Compound bilingualism** ☐☐☐

015 **Comprehensible input** ☐☐☐

016 **Comprehensible output hypothesis** ☐☐☐

017 **Contrastive Analysis Hypothesis (CAH)** ☐☐☐

018 **Controlled processes / processing** ☐☐☐

019 **Conversation Analysis (CA)** ☐☐☐

020 **Coordinate bilingualism** ☐☐☐

021 **Critical period hypothesis** ☐☐☐

022 Cross-linguistic Influence (CLI) □□□

023 Declarative knowledge □□□

024 Discourse analysis □□□

025 Display question(s) □□□

026 Drill □□□

027 Elicitation □□□

028 Ellipsis (related to cohesion) □□□

029 Error analysis □□□

030 Explicit knowledge □□□

031 Facilitation □□□

032 Feedback type □□□
  ① explicit correction □□□
  ② recast □□□
  ③ clarification request □□□

④ metalinguistic feedback ☐☐☐

⑤ elicitation ☐☐☐

⑥ repetition ☐☐☐

033 **Fossilization** ☐☐☐

034 **Grammar consciousness raising** ☐☐☐

035 **Halliday's seven functions of language (Developmental functions of language)** ☐☐☐

① Instrumental ☐☐☐

② Regulatory ☐☐☐

③ Interactional ☐☐☐

④ Personal ☐☐☐

⑤ Heuristic ☐☐☐

⑥ Imaginative ☐☐☐

⑦ Informative ☐☐☐

036 **Idiosyncratic dialect** ☐☐☐

037 **Implicit knowledge** ☐☐☐

038 **Indicator (Varonis and Gass's (1985) model of negotiation)** □□□

039 **Input hypothesis** □□□

040 **Input** □□□

041 **Intake** □□□

042 **Integrated approach / skills** □□□

043 **Interaction hypothesis** □□□

044 **Interface hypothesis** □□□
① non-interface position □□□
② strong interface position □□□
③ weak interface position □□□

045 **Interference** □□□

046 **Interlingual transfer** □□□

047 **Internalization** □□□

048 **Intralingual transfer** □□□

⁰⁴⁹ **Lexical cohesion** ☐☐☐
(related to cohesion)

⁰⁵⁰ **Markedness differential** ☐☐☐
hypothesis
(=Markedness theory)

⁰⁵¹ **Meaningful learning** ☐☐☐

⁰⁵² **Modified input** ☐☐☐

⁰⁵³ **Modified interaction** ☐☐☐

⁰⁵⁴ **Modified output** ☐☐☐

⁰⁵⁵ **Monitor hypothesis** ☐☐☐

⁰⁵⁶ **Multiple intelligences** ☐☐☐

⁰⁵⁷ **Negative evidence** ☐☐☐

⁰⁵⁸ **Negative transfer** ☐☐☐

⁰⁵⁹ **Negotiation of form** ☐☐☐

060 Negotiation of meaning (=meaning-negotiation strategies) ☐☐☐

① comprehension check ☐☐☐

② clarification request ☐☐☐

③ confirmation check ☐☐☐

061 Noticing hypothesis ☐☐☐

062 Noticing the gap ☐☐☐

063 Overgeneralization ☐☐☐

064 Personalization ☐☐☐

065 Positive evidence ☐☐☐

066 Positive transfer ☐☐☐

067 Pragmalinguistics ☐☐☐

068 Procedural knowledge ☐☐☐

069 Psycholinguistics ☐☐☐

070 Pushed output ☐☐☐

**071 Reaction to response
(Varonis and Gass's (1985)
model of negotiation)** ☐☐☐

072 Recast ☐☐☐

**073 Reference
(related to cohesion)** ☐☐☐

074 Referential question(s) ☐☐☐

075 Regulation ☐☐☐

076 Rehearsal ☐☐☐

077 Repair ☐☐☐

078 Repetition ☐☐☐

**079 Response
(Varonis and Gass's (1985)
model of negotiation)** ☐☐☐

**080 Rote learning
(≒Rote memorizing)** ☐☐☐

081 **Scaffolding** ☐☐☐

082 **Schematic knowledge (cf. schemata)** ☐☐☐

083 **Self-regulation** ☐☐☐

084 **Silent period** ☐☐☐

085 **Sociocultural Theory (SCT)** ☐☐☐

086 **Substitution (related to cohesion)** ☐☐☐

087 **Subtractive bilingualism** ☐☐☐

088 **Trigger (Varonis and Gass's (1985) model of negotiation)** ☐☐☐

089 **Turn-taking** ☐☐☐

090 **U-shaped acquisition / development / learning** ☐☐☐

091 **Unanalyzed language** ☐☐☐

092 **Uptake** ☐☐☐

093 **Whole language education** ☐☐☐

094 **Zone of Proximal
Development (ZPD)** ☐☐☐

Learner-related Terms
(Learning Strategies, Styles, Variables & Interlanguage)

Check

001 **Affective filter**
(by Stephan Krashen)

002 **Affective strategy(ies)**

003 **Agency**

004 **Ambiguity intolerance**

005 **Ambiguity tolerance**
(tolerance of ambiguity)

006 **Amotivation**

007 **Anxiety**

008 **Auditory learning style**

009 **Avoidance**

010 **Cognitive strategies**

[011] **Cognitive style** ☐☐☐

[012] **Collaboration** ☐☐☐

[013] **Communication strategies** ☐☐☐
 (Dörnyei, 1995)

[014] **Compensatory strategies** ☐☐☐
 (communication strategies)
 ① avoidance ☐☐☐
 ② circumlocution ☐☐☐
 ③ approximation ☐☐☐
 ④ word coinage ☐☐☐
 ⑤ prefabricated patterns ☐☐☐
 ⑥ code-switching ☐☐☐
 ⑦ appeal to authority ☐☐☐
 ⑧ literal translation ☐☐☐
 ⑨ keeping the floor ☐☐☐
 ⑩ foreignizing ☐☐☐
 ⑪ nonlinguistic signals ☐☐☐

[015] **Contrastive analysis** ☐☐☐

[016] **Covert error(s)** ☐☐☐

017 **Debilitative anxiety**　☐☐☐

018 **Demotivation**　☐☐☐

019 **Difficulty**　☐☐☐

020 **Emergent stage**　☐☐☐

021 **Emotional intelligence (EQ, Emotional Quotient)**　☐☐☐

022 **Empathy**　☐☐☐

023 **Equilibration**　☐☐☐

024 **Errors of addition, omission, substitution, and permutation**　☐☐☐

025 **Extrinsic motivation**　☐☐☐

026 **Extroversion**　☐☐☐

027 **Facilitative anxiety**　☐☐☐

028 **Field Dependence (FD)**　☐☐☐

029 **Field Independence (FI)**　☐☐☐

030 **Field sensitivity** ☐☐☐

031 **Global error(s)** ☐☐☐

032 **Global self-esteem** ☐☐☐

033 **High Input Generators (HIGs)** ☐☐☐

034 **Hypercorrection** ☐☐☐

035 **Identity** ☐☐☐

036 **Impulsivity (impulsive style)** ☐☐☐

037 **Induced error(s)** ☐☐☐

038 **Inhibition** ☐☐☐

039 **Instrumental orientation** ☐☐☐

040 **Integrative orientation** ☐☐☐

041 **Interactional competence** ☐☐☐

042 **Intercultural competence** ☐☐☐

043 **Interlanguage** ☐☐☐

044 **Interlingual transfer** ☐☐☐

045 **Intralingual transfer** ☐☐☐

046 **Intrinsic motivation** ☐☐☐

047 **Introversion** ☐☐☐

048 **Kinesthetic learning style** ☐☐☐

049 **Language anxiety** ☐☐☐

050 **Language ego** ☐☐☐

051 **Learnability** ☐☐☐

052 **Learning strategies** ☐☐☐

053 **Learning style** ☐☐☐

054 **Left-brain dominance** ☐☐☐

055 **Local error(s)** ☐☐☐

056 **Low Input Generators (LIGs)** ☐☐☐

⁰⁵⁷ **Metacognitive strategy(ies)** □□□

⁰⁵⁸ **Orientation** □□□

⁰⁵⁹ **Overt error(s)** □□□

⁰⁶⁰ **Peer pressure** □□□

⁰⁶¹ **Postsystematic stage** □□□

⁰⁶² **Prefabricated patterns** □□□

⁰⁶³ **Presystematic (error)** □□□

⁰⁶⁴ **Proactive inhibition** □□□

⁰⁶⁵ **Rapport** □□□

⁰⁶⁶ **Reflectivity (reflective style)** □□□

⁰⁶⁷ **Retroactive inhibition** □□□

⁰⁶⁸ **Right-brain dominance** □□□

⁰⁶⁹ **Risk taking** □□□

⁰⁷⁰ **Second identity** □□□

071 **Self-actualization** ☐☐☐

072 **Self-correction** ☐☐☐

073 **Self-determination** ☐☐☐

074 **Self-efficacy** ☐☐☐

075 **Self-esteem** ☐☐☐

076 **Self-regulation** ☐☐☐

077 **Situation self-esteem** ☐☐☐

078 **Socioaffective strategies** ☐☐☐

079 **Sociocultural-interactive (S-I)** ☐☐☐
strategy

080 **Sociolinguistic competence** ☐☐☐
(≒sociocultural competence)

081 **Stabilization** ☐☐☐

082 **State anxiety** ☐☐☐

083 **Strategic competence** ☐☐☐

⁰⁸⁴ **Strategic self-regulation (S²R)** ☐☐☐

⁰⁸⁵ **Systematicity** ☐☐☐

⁰⁸⁶ **Task self-esteem** ☐☐☐

⁰⁸⁷ **Tolerance of ambiguity** ☐☐☐

⁰⁸⁸ **Trait anxiety** ☐☐☐

⁰⁸⁹ **Variation(=variability)** ☐☐☐

⁰⁹⁰ **Visual, auditory, tactile, kinesthetic learning styles** ☐☐☐

⁰⁹¹ **Willingness To Communicate (WTC)** ☐☐☐

⁰⁹² **Working memory** ☐☐☐

Teaching-related Terms

(Teaching Culture, Materials & Methods & Communicative Competence)

Check

001 **Acculturation**

002 **Acculturation model**

003 **Action research**

004 **Adjunct model (of content-based language teaching)**

005 **Anomie**

006 **Artifact(s)**

007 **Artifact study**

008 **Audiolingual Method (ALM)**

009 **Audio-motor unit**

010 **Autonomy**

011 **Blended learning** ☐☐☐

012 **Communicative task (Prahbu, 1987)** ☐☐☐

013 **Community Language Learning (CLL)** ☐☐☐

014 **Computer-adaptive Testing (CAT) (=tailored testing)** ☐☐☐

015 **Computer-assisted Language Learning (CALL)** ☐☐☐

016 **Computer-mediated Communication (CMC)** ☐☐☐

017 **Concordance** ☐☐☐

018 **Concordancing** ☐☐☐

019 **Content-based Instruction (CBI)/Content-based Language Teaching (CBLT)** ☐☐☐

① **Immersion model** ☐☐☐

② **Sheltered model** ☐☐☐
    (sheltered-language instruction)

③ **Adjunct model** ☐☐☐

④ **Theme-based instruction** ☐☐☐

020 **Cooperative learning** ☐☐☐

021 **Corpus linguistics** ☐☐☐

022 **Corpus-based teaching** ☐☐☐

023 **Culture assimilator** ☐☐☐

024 **Culture capsule** ☐☐☐

025 **Culture island** ☐☐☐

026 **Culture shock** ☐☐☐

027 **Culture stress** ☐☐☐

028 **Digital literacy** ☐☐☐

029 **Direct method** ☐☐☐

030 **Discovery learning** ☐☐☐

031 **Elaboration** ☐☐☐

032 **English only (debate)** ☐☐☐

033 **Experiential learning** ☐☐☐

034 **Eye contact** ☐☐☐

035 **Flipped learning** ☐☐☐

036 **Functional syllabus** ☐☐☐

037 **Group dynamics** ☐☐☐

038 **Immersion** ☐☐☐

039 **Inner circle** ☐☐☐

040 **Input modification** ☐☐☐

041 **Kinesics** ☐☐☐

042 **Kinesthetics** ☐☐☐

043 **Language competence (Bachman, 1990)** ☐☐☐

044 **Learner-centered instruction** □□□

045 **Lexical approach** □□□

046 **Lexico-grammatical approach** □□□

047 **Metalanguage** □□□

048 **Mobil-assisted Language Learning (MALL)** □□□

049 **Modified input** □□□
   ① simplication □□□
   ② elaboration □□□

050 **Multimodal communication** □□□

051 **Native informant** □□□

052 **Natural approach** □□□

053 **Needs analysis / Needs assessment** □□□

⁰⁵⁴ **Notional-functional syllabus** ☐☐☐
  (=functional syllabus)

⁰⁵⁵ **Objective needs** ☐☐☐

⁰⁵⁶ **Oculesics** ☐☐☐

⁰⁵⁷ **Olfactory** ☐☐☐

⁰⁵⁸ **Optimal distance model** ☐☐☐

⁰⁵⁹ **Outer circle** ☐☐☐

⁰⁶⁰ **Pair work** ☐☐☐

⁰⁶¹ **Pedagogical task(s)** ☐☐☐
  (=pedagogic task(s))

⁰⁶² **PPP: Presentation →** ☐☐☐
  Practice → Production

⁰⁶³ **Perceived social distance** ☐☐☐

⁰⁶⁴ **Process-oriented syllabus** ☐☐☐

⁰⁶⁵ **Product-oriented syllabus** ☐☐☐

066 Project-based Learning (PBL) ☐☐☐

067 Psychological distance ☐☐☐

068 Realia ☐☐☐

069 Sheltered model (sheltered-language instruction) ☐☐☐

070 Simplification ☐☐☐

071 Social distance ☐☐☐

072 Sociocultural awareness ☐☐☐

073 Sociopragmatics ☐☐☐

074 Speech acts ☐☐☐

075 Spiral learning ☐☐☐

076 Strategies-based Instruction (SBI) ☐☐☐

077 Structural syllabus ☐☐☐

078 **Subject-integrated class** □□□

079 **Subjective needs** □□□

080 **Sustained Deep Learning (SDL)** □□□

081 **Target task(s)** □□□

082 **Task-based Language Teaching (TBLT)** □□□

083 **Teachability hypothesis** □□□

084 **Teacher-centered instruction** □□□

085 **Teacher's roles (From the most directive role to less directive)** □□□
  ① Controller □□□
  ② Director □□□
  ③ Manager □□□
  ④ Facilitator □□□
  ⑤ Resource □□□

086 Textbook adaptation
   ① adding
   ② deleting
   ③ modifying
   ④ simplifying
   ⑤ reordering

087 Theme-based instruction

088 Think-aloud strategy / technique

089 Total Physical Response (TPR)

090 Translanguaging

091 Uncertainty avoidance

092 World Englishes

Listening

	Check
001 **Bottom-up processing**	☐☐☐
002 **Contextual knowledge**	☐☐☐
003 **Chunk / Chunking (clustering)**	☐☐☐
004 **Dictogloss**	☐☐☐
005 **Extensive listening (listening for pleasure)**	☐☐☐
006 **Inferential listening**	☐☐☐
007 **Information transfer**	☐☐☐
008 **Intensive listening (listening for a purpose)**	☐☐☐
009 **Interpersonal dialogue**	☐☐☐

010 Jigsaw listening ☐☐☐

011 Listening for details ☐☐☐

012 Listening for gist ☐☐☐

013 Monitoring ☐☐☐

014 Predicting ☐☐☐

015 Reduced forms ☐☐☐

016 Redundancy ☐☐☐

017 Scanning ☐☐☐

018 Top-down processing ☐☐☐

019 Transactional dialogue ☐☐☐

Reading

Check ✎

001 **Advance organizer** ☐☐☐

002 **Basal readers (Basal approach, Bottom-up)** ☐☐☐

003 **Bottom-up (data-driven) processing** ☐☐☐

004 **Content schemata** ☐☐☐

005 **Contextual knowledge** ☐☐☐

006 **Discourse markers** ☐☐☐

007 **Exploitability (for choosing reading texts)** ☐☐☐

008 **Extensive reading** ☐☐☐

009 **Formal schemata** ☐☐☐

010 **Graded reader(s)** ☐☐☐

011 **Graphic Organizer (GO)** ☐☐☐

012 **Guessing** ☐☐☐

013 **Inferencing** ☐☐☐

014 **Intensive reading** ☐☐☐

015 **Interactive processing** ☐☐☐

016 **Language Experience** ☐☐☐
Approach (LEA, 1967)
(Top-down)

017 **Linguistic approach** ☐☐☐
(Bottom-up)

018 **Literature-based approach** ☐☐☐
(Top-down)

019 **Readability (for choosing** ☐☐☐
reading texts)

020 **Scanning** □□□

021 **Schema theory** □□□

022 **Schemata** □□□

023 **Semantic mapping /
Clustering** □□□

024 **Skimming** □□□

025 **SQ3R** □□□

026 **Suitability of content (for
choosing reading texts)** □□□

027 **Top-down (concept-driven)
processing** □□□

Speaking & Pronunciation

	Check
001 **Accuracy** (in terms of speaking skills)	☐☐☐
002 **Adjacency pair** (in conversation analysis)	☐☐☐
003 **Attention getting**	☐☐☐
004 **Chunk / Chunking** (clustering)	☐☐☐
005 **Conversational gambits**	☐☐☐
006 **Discourse**	☐☐☐
007 **Discourse competence** (one of communicative competence)	☐☐☐
008 **Formality**	☐☐☐

009 **Fluency** ☐☐☐

010 **Grammatical competence (or linguistic competence, one of communicative competence)** ☐☐☐

011 **Haptics** ☐☐☐

012 **Illocutionary competence** ☐☐☐

013 **Illocutionary force** ☐☐☐

014 **Information exchange** ☐☐☐

015 **Information gap activity** ☐☐☐

016 **Intelligibility** ☐☐☐

017 **Jigsaw** ☐☐☐

018 **Meaningful minimal pairs** ☐☐☐

019 **Metalinguistic explanation** ☐☐☐

020 **Minimal pairs** ☐☐☐

021 Negotiation of meaning
　① comprehension check
　② clarification request
　③ confirmation check

022 Oral dialogue journals

023 Perlocutionary force

024 Picture description task

025 Pragmatic competence

026 Register

027 Rehearsal

028 Role-play(s)

029 Role(s)

**030 Segmentals
(teaching pronunciation)**

031 Shifting (of a topic)

032 **Simulation(s)** □□□

033 **Sociolinguistic competence (one of communicative competence)** □□□

034 **Speech styles** □□□
 ① Frozen style □□□
 ② Formal style □□□
 ③ Consultative style □□□
 ④ Casual style □□□
 ⑤ Intimate style □□□

035 **Storytelling** □□□

036 **Strategic competence (one of communicative competence)** □□□

037 **Styles (in speech discourse)** □□□

038 **Suprasegmentals (teaching pronunciation)** □□□

039 Task type (Richard, 2001) ☐☐☐
   ① Jigsaw ☐☐☐
   ② Information-gap ☐☐☐
   ③ Problem-solving ☐☐☐
   ④ Decision-making ☐☐☐
   ⑤ Opinion exchange ☐☐☐

040 Termination (of a topic) ☐☐☐

041 Topic clarification ☐☐☐

042 Topic development ☐☐☐

043 Topic nomination ☐☐☐

044 Turn-taking ☐☐☐

Writing

	Check
001 **Brainstorming**	☐☐☐
002 **Checklist**	☐☐☐
003 **Conference(ing)**	☐☐☐
004 **Controlled writing**	☐☐☐
005 **Dialogue journal(s)**	☐☐☐
006 **Dictocomp / Dicto-composition**	☐☐☐
007 **Discourse**	☐☐☐
008 **Display writing**	☐☐☐
009 **Error Correction Code (ECC)**	☐☐☐

010 **Formality** ☐☐☐

011 **Freewriting** ☐☐☐

012 **Genre** ☐☐☐

013 **Genre-based approach / writing** ☐☐☐

014 **Guided writing** ☐☐☐

015 **Intercultural rhetoric** ☐☐☐

016 **Peer-editing** ☐☐☐

017 **Process-oriented approach** ☐☐☐

018 **Product-oriented approach** ☐☐☐

019 **Real writing** ☐☐☐

020 **Rhetorical formality (in writing)** ☐☐☐

021 **Self-writing** ☐☐☐

022 **Sentence combining** ☐☐☐

Vocabulary & Grammar

	Check
001 **Abductive approach**	☐☐☐
002 **Accuracy**	☐☐☐
003 **Appropriateness**	☐☐☐
004 **Attention**	☐☐☐
005 **Breadth of knowledge**	☐☐☐
006 **Collocation**	☐☐☐
007 **Complexity**	☐☐☐
008 **Concordance**	☐☐☐
009 **Concordancer**	☐☐☐
010 **Concordancing**	☐☐☐
011 **Connotation**	☐☐☐

012 **Consciousness-raising task (CR task)** □□□

013 **Corpora** □□□

014 **Corpus linguistics** □□□

015 **Declarative knowledge** □□□

016 **Deductive approach** □□□

017 **Depth of knowledge** □□□

018 **Dictogloss** □□□

019 **Drill(s)** □□□

020 **Explicit instruction** □□□

021 **Explicit knowledge** □□□

022 **Explicit (treatment of form)** □□□

023 **Focus on Form (FonF)** □□□

024 **Focus on Forms (FonFs)** □□□

025	**Focus on meaning**	☐☐☐
026	**Form (of language)**	☐☐☐
027	**Form-focused Instruction (FFI)**	☐☐☐
028	**Frequency**	☐☐☐
029	**Garden path**	☐☐☐
030	**Global error(s)**	☐☐☐
031	**Grammaring**	☐☐☐
032	**Hypercorrection**	☐☐☐
033	**Implicit instruction**	☐☐☐
034	**Implicit knowledge**	☐☐☐
035	**Implicit learning**	☐☐☐
036	**Implicit (treatment of form)**	☐☐☐
037	**Incidental learning**	☐☐☐

038 **Inductive approach** ☐☐☐

039 **Input enhancement** ☐☐☐

040 **Input flooding** ☐☐☐

041 **Input processing** ☐☐☐

042 **Intentional learning** ☐☐☐

043 **Keyword method / technique** ☐☐☐

044 **Lexical approach** ☐☐☐

045 **Lexicogrammatical approach** ☐☐☐

046 **Local error(s)** ☐☐☐

047 **Meaningful drill(s)** ☐☐☐

048 **Mechanical drill(s)** ☐☐☐

049 **PPP (presentation, practice, production)** ☐☐☐

050 **Procedural knowledge** ☐☐☐

051 **Processing instruction** □□□

052 **Productive knowledge** □□□

053 **Receptive knowledge** □□□

054 **Restructuring** □□□

055 **Salience** □□□

056 **Structured input** □□□

057 **Structured input activities** □□□

058 **Structured output** □□□

059 **Teachability hypothesis** □□□

060 **Vocabulary analysis (=word analysis)** □□□

061 **Word family(ies)** □□□

062 **Word formation** □□□

063 **Word map** □□□

Assessment & Test

Check ✎

001 **Achievement test** ☐☐☐

002 **Alternative assessment
(e.g. portfolios, journals,
self- and peer-assessment)** ☐☐☐

003 **Analytic scoring method** ☐☐☐

004 **Appropriate word scoring
(acceptable word method)
(in Cloze test)** ☐☐☐

005 **Authentic assessment** ☐☐☐

006 **Authenticity (of a test)** ☐☐☐

007 **Cloze test** ☐☐☐

008 **Concurrent validity** □□□

009 **Construct validity** □□□

010 **Content validity** □□□

011 **Criterion validity** □□□

012 **Criterion-referenced test** □□□

013 **C-test (related to Cloze test)** □□□

014 **Diagnostic test** □□□

015 **Direct test** □□□

016 **Discrete point testing (e.g., multiple-choice, grammar item)** □□□

017 **Distractor (efficiency) analysis** □□□

018 **Electronic portfolio (e-portfolio)** □□□

019 Exact word method
(in Cloze test) □□□

020 Face validity □□□

021 Fixed-ratio deletion
(in Cloze test) □□□

022 Formal assessment □□□

023 Formative assessment / test □□□

024 Holistic scoring method □□□

025 Indirect test □□□

026 Informal assessment □□□

027 Integrative testing
(e.g., interviews, Cloze test) □□□

028 Internal consistency
(reliability) □□□

029 Inter-rater reliability □□□

030 **Intra-rater reliability** ☐☐☐

031 **Item difficulty** ☐☐☐

032 **Item discrimination** ☐☐☐

033 **Item facility**
(=item difficulty) ☐☐☐

034 **Journals** ☐☐☐

035 **Norm-referenced test** ☐☐☐

036 **Objective test (e.g., multiple-** ☐☐☐
choice, true or false answers,
matching questions)

037 **Performance assessment** ☐☐☐
(performance-based
assessment)

038 **Placement test** ☐☐☐

039 **Portfolio(s)** ☐☐☐

040 **Practicality** ☐☐☐

041 **Predictive validity** ☐☐☐

042 **Proficiency test** ☐☐☐

043 **Rational deletion**
(in Cloze test) ☐☐☐

044 **Reliability** ☐☐☐

045 **Rubrics** ☐☐☐

046 **Self- and peer- assessment** ☐☐☐

047 **Student-related reliability** ☐☐☐

048 **Subjective test (e.g., extended-**
response questions, essays) ☐☐☐

049 **Summative assessment / test** ☐☐☐

050 **Test reliability** ☐☐☐

051 **Validity** ☐☐☐

052 **Washback** ☐☐☐

교원임용시험 전공영어대비

KEYTERM MASTER

for EFL teachers

Song Eun Woo

동영상강의 박문각임용 www.pmg.co.kr

별책부록 **KEYTERM 미니북**

머리말

안녕하세요. 영어교육론을 사랑하는 여러분! 오늘도 즐겁게 공부하고 계신가요?

지난해 처음으로 출간한 《Keyterm Master》의 제2판을 출간하게 되었습니다. 단 1년 만에 2판을 제작하게 되어 그동안 영어교육론을 공부하는 많은 분이 한 권으로 정리된 key terms 용어집의 필요성을 얼마나 느꼈는지 알 수 있었습니다. 이에 우리 임용준비생 여러분들이 《Keyterm Master》를 활용하여 짧은 시간 동안 key terms와 key phrases를 마스터할 수 있도록 더 큰 책임감을 느끼면서 더 발전하고 견고해진 《Keyterm Master》 제2판을 제작하였습니다.

영어교육론을 공부하는 과정에서 가장 우선으로 해야 할 것은 바로 key terms와 key phrases에 대한 정확한 이해와 암기입니다. 그러나 영어교육론에 관한 공부가 충분히 이루어지지 않은 상황에서 여러분 각자가 수많은 key terms를 직접 찾고 그 배경을 이해하기에는 한계가 분명히 존재합니다. 또한 시대별 영어교육 경향에 맞춰 새로운 terms가 생성되고 기존의 terms가 다른 용어로 대체되는 것은 임용준비생들에게 더 큰 어려움으로 다가옵니다. 따라서 주제별로 분류한 최신 key terms를 중요도에 맞춰 여러 번 반복·학습할 수 있도록 도와주는 《Keyterm Master》를 활용하는 것이 최단 시간에 최대 효율을 낼 수 있는 효과적인 key terms 정복의 길이라고 생각합니다. 또한 key terms가 포함하고 있는 핵심 의미, 즉 key phrases를 동시에 학습하지 않으면 자칫 해당 용어에 대한 잘못된 이해를 하게 될 수 있기 때문에 필수적으로 key phrases를 함께 학습해야 합니다. 아울러 key phrases에 대한 학습은 여러분들이 문항 내 데이터를 분석하거나 답안을 작성할 때, 감점으로 이어지지 않도록 정확도를 높여줄 수 있는 핵심 전략입니다.

제한적인 학습 시간으로 인해 학습 전략의 선택이 승패를 좌우하는 임용시험인 만큼 최대한 빠르고 효율적으로 key terms와 key phrases에 익숙해지는 것이 더 탄탄한 기초를 가지고 다음 단계로 빠르게 나아갈 수 있는 유일한 방법입니다. 물론 한 번의 학습이 완벽한 암기와 이해로 이어질 수는 없습니다. 하지만 한 번의 학습도 유의미한 학습이 될 수 있도록 《Keyterm Master》에서는 3단계의 학습 방법을 제시합니다. 각 단계별 학습 방법은 다음에 나오는 How to use this book에 자세히 기술하였으니 꼼꼼히 읽어 본 뒤, 최대의 효율로 공부하시기 바랍니다. Preview, Definitions, Review, (+ Minibook)을 통해 학습하다 보면 어느새 여러분은 많고 어려웠던 key terms & key phrases에 친숙해지고 자연스러운 이해와 암기가 완성된 것을 경험할 수 있을 것입니다.

지금 당장은 key terms가 너무 많아 추상적이고 이해하기 힘들어서 나를 괴롭게 하는 부분이라고 생각될 수 있습니다. 하지만 여러분이 영어교육론 key terms를 정복할 수 있다는 사실을 믿고 《Keyterm Master》와 함께 체계적인 반복 · 학습을 하다 보면 그 어떤 어려운 공부도 극복하고 해낼 수 있다는 것을 느끼게 될 것입니다. 여러분이 영어교사의 꿈에 더 쉽게 가까이 다가갈 수 있게, 할 수 있다는 믿음을 가질 수 있게, 그렇게 꿈을 이룬 여러분 한 분 한 분이 더 좋은 교사가 되어 즐겁고 재미있는 영어교육 환경을 만들어가는 주역이 될 것이라는 믿음을 가지고 정성껏 제작하였다는 말씀을 드리면서 이 글을 마칩니다.

Teaching is a noble profession that shapes the character, intellect, and souls of future generations.

–St. Elizabeth Ann Seton

영어교육론 송은우

How to use
this book

1. Preview

Key Terms를 본격적으로 학습하기 전 여러분이 미리 Key Terms를 확인하고 각각의 뜻을 예측해 볼 수 있도록 Preview 단계를 제시합니다. Preview 단계에서 나에게 익숙한 용어와 낯선 용어를 먼저 구분한 뒤, 낯선 용어에 관해서는 예상되는 뜻과 의미, 상황을 먼저 생각해 본 후, 해당 용어를 학습하는 두 번째 단계로 넘어갑니다.

> ☐   Additive bilingualism
> ☐   Affective filter hypothesis
> ☐   Analyzed languages

2. Definitions & Key Phrases

Definitions & Key Phrases를 본격적으로 다루는 두 번째 단계에서는 각 용어마다 나의 예측이 잘 맞았는지, 어긋난 부분이 있는지 확인합니다. 예측이 잘 맞았다면 꼼꼼히 읽어보며 혹시 추가적으로 더 중요한 부분은 없는지 확인하고 어긋난 부분이 있다면 역시 그 부분도 확인합니다. (예측이 어긋났다고 속상해 할 필요 없습니다. 실질적으로 나의 예상에서 벗어날 때, 학습이 더 잘 이루어질 수도 있습니다. ^^)

더불어, Key Terms의 '정의' 및 '실제 상황과 관련된 의미'를 정리합니다. Key Terms를 이해하는 데 도움이 되는 핵심 Phrases가 밑줄 쳐져 있으니 반드시 확인하고 이해 및 기억하도록 합니다. 또한, 별표(★)를 이용하여 중요도에 따른 표시도 제공되니 꼭! 확인하면서 학습합니다. 처음부터 모든 Key Terms를 기억하기는 쉽지 않을 수 있으니 가장 중요한 것부터 학습하면서 점차 Key Terms의 양을 확장해 나가는 것도 효과적인 학습 방법입니다.

중요도: 중등교사 임용시험(영어) 기출빈도를 고려하여 현재 영어교육론 안에서 화두가 되는 정도에 따라 분류하였습니다.

매우 중요	★★★
중요	★★★
보통	★★★
영어교육론 이해 전반에 필요한 기초용어	ⓑ (Basic)
용어 확장을 위한 참고용어	ⓔ (Extra)

01   Acquisition-learning hypothesis★★★

It states that there are two types of development. **Acquisition** is the developı implicit L2 knowledge that can be used to produce language in real time. Leaı

3. Review Quiz

본론 부분이 충분히 숙지되었다면 마지막 Review 단계를 진행합니다. Review Quiz에서는 앞서 학습한 Key Terms의 일부를 퀴즈로 제시하였습니다. 주어진 Key Phrases를 읽으면서 Key Terms를 적어보고 나의 Key Terms에 대한 이해와 암기 정도를 확인합니다. Key Terms의 스펠링도 완벽하게 암기하고 있어야 하기 때문에 여러 번 손으로 적어보는 것을 추천합니다. 실제 시험에서 갑자기 스펠링이 헷갈리는 경우가 있을 수 있으므로 손에서부터 익숙하게 만드는 것이 실전 시험에서 큰 도움이 될 수 있습니다. (특히, 접미사 -ed, -tive, -er, -tion 등이 헷갈리기 쉽습니다.)

> ※ **Read the following descriptions and fill in the blanks.**
>
> 01 _____ _____ **hypothesis**
>
> It states that input can only become intake if learners have a low filter, that say if they view the target language and the learning context favorably. If have high filter, then their resistance towards the language will interfere

4. Note

챕터별 Key Terms를 복기하거나 각자 추가하고 싶은 Key Terms가 있다면 적어두는 용도로 활용 가능합니다.

5. Index

본 교재에 포함된 모든 Key Terms를 Index에 알파벳순으로 정리하였습니다. Key Terms 학습을 하는 도중 헷갈리는 Terms가 있다면 Index에서 Page를 찾아 다시 한 번 Definitions과 Key Phrases를 확인하고 학습합니다.

6. Minibook

본 교재에 포함된 챕터별 Key Terms를 미니북으로 제작하여 언제 어디서든 손쉽게 나의 학습 정도를 확인할 수 있습니다. 1) Preview 2) Definitions & Key Phrases 3) Review의 3단계를 거쳐서 학습한 Key Terms라 할지라도 단 일주일이라도 덮어두고 보지 않으면 일부는 기억에서 사라지기 마련입니다. 그러므로 언제, 어디서든 간편하게 Key Terms를 복습할 수 있는 MINIBOOK을 활용하도록 합니다. 챕터별 Key Terms를 틈틈이 복습하고 내가 이미 습득한 Terms와 아직 개념이 명확하지 않은 Key Terms를 여러 번 확인하여 Key Terms를 마스터 해봅시다.

Contents

목차

Chapter 01 Basic Concepts and Perspectives in SLA   10
(Principles & Models)

Chapter 02 Learner-related Terms   56
(Learning Strategies, Styles, Variables &
Interlanguage)

Chapter 03 Teaching-related Terms   94
(Teaching Culture, Materials & Methods,
Communicative Competence)

Chapter 04 Listening   146

Chapter 05 Reading   160

Chapter 06   Speaking & Pronunciation   182

Chapter 07   Writing   208

Chapter 08   Vocabulary & Grammar   224

Chapter 09   Assessment & Test   266

Index   300

Basic Concepts and Perspectives in SLA

(Principles & Models)

※ **Review the following Key Terms list and put a checkmark next to Terms that you do not know the exact meaning.**

- ☐ Acquisition-learning hypothesis
- ☐ Additive bilingualism
- ☐ Affective filter hypothesis
- ☐ Analyzed language
- ☐ Anomie
- ☐ Audiolingualism
- ☐ Automatic processes / Automaticity
- ☐ Backsliding
- ☐ Behaviorism
- ☐ Bilingualism
- ☐ Coherence
- ☐ Cohesion
- ☐ Communicative Language Teaching (CLT)
- ☐ Competence
- ☐ Compound bilingualism
- ☐ Comprehensible input
- ☐ Comprehensible output hypothesis
- ☐ Comprehension
- ☐ Conscious learning
- ☐ Contrastive Analysis Hypothesis (CAH)
- ☐ Controlled processes
- ☐ Conversation Analysis (CA)
- ☐ Conversational interactions
- ☐ Coordinate bilingualism
- ☐ Critical period hypothesis

- [ ] Cross-linguistic Influence (CLI)
- [ ] Declarative knowledge
- [ ] Discourse analysis
- [ ] Display question
- [ ] Drill
- [ ] Elicitation
- [ ] Ellipsis
- [ ] English as a Foreign Language (EFL)
- [ ] English as a Second Language (ESL)
- [ ] English as an International Language (EIL)
- [ ] Error analysis
- [ ] Explicit knowledge
- [ ] Facilitation
- [ ] Feedback type   ① explicit correction   ② recast   ③ clarification request
  ④ metalinguistic feedback   ⑤ elicitation   ⑥ repetition
- [ ] Fossilization
- [ ] Grammar consciousness raising
- [ ] Halliday's seven functions of language
- [ ] Hierarchy of difficulty
- [ ] Idiosyncratic dialect
- [ ] Implicit knowledge
- [ ] Input
- [ ] Input hypothesis
- [ ] Intake
- [ ] Integrated approach / skills
- [ ] Interaction hypothesis
- [ ] Interface hypothesis   ① non-interface position   ② strong interface position
  ③ weak interface position
- [ ] Interference

- ☐ Interlingual transfer
- ☐ Internalization
- ☐ Intralingual transfer
- ☐ Language Acquisition Device (LAD)
- ☐ Lexical cohesion (related to cohesion)
- ☐ Markedness differential hypothesis (=Markedness theory)
- ☐ Meaningful learning
- ☐ Modified input ① simplification ② elaboration
- ☐ Modified interaction
- ☐ Modified output
- ☐ Monitor hypothesis
- ☐ Motivation ① integrative ② instrumental ③ intrinsic ④ extrinsic
- ☐ Multiple intelligences
- ☐ Natural order hypothesis
- ☐ Negative evidence
- ☐ Negative transfer
- ☐ Negotiation of form
- ☐ Negotiation of meaning (=meaning-negotiation strategies)
  ① comprehension check ② clarification request ③ confirmation check
- ☐ Noticing hypothesis
- ☐ Noticing the gap
- ☐ Output
- ☐ Overgeneralization
- ☐ Performance
- ☐ Personalization
- ☐ Positive evidence
- ☐ Positive transfer
- ☐ Pragmalinguistics
- ☐ Procedural knowledge

- ☐ Proficiency
- ☐ Psycholinguistics
- ☐ Pushed output
- ☐ Reaction to response
- ☐ Recast
- ☐ Referential question
- ☐ Regulation
- ☐ Rehearsal
- ☐ Repair
- ☐ Repetition
- ☐ Response
- ☐ Rote learning
- ☐ Scaffolding
- ☐ Schematic knowledge (cf. schemata)
- ☐ Second Language Acquisition (SLA)
- ☐ Self-regulation
- ☐ Silent period
- ☐ Sociocultural Theory (SCT)
- ☐ Substitution (related to cohesion)
- ☐ Subtractive bilingualism
- ☐ Transfer
- ☐ Trigger
- ☐ Turn-taking
- ☐ U-shaped acquisition / development / learning
- ☐ Unanalyzed language
- ☐ Universal Grammar (UG)
- ☐ Uptake
- ☐ Whole language education
- ☐ Zone of Proximal Development (ZPD)

01 Acquisition***

It occurs <u>subconsciously</u> as a result of <u>participating in natural communication</u> where the focus is on <u>meaning</u>. (Learning, which refers to conscious processes that result in explicit knowledge about the grammar properties of a second language. Thus, **acquired knowledge** serves as the major source for initiating both the comprehension and production of utterances. **Learnt knowledge** is available for use only by the monitor. Learning cannot lead to acquisition.)

02 Acquisition-learning hypothesis***

It states that there are two types of development. **Acquisition** is the development of <u>implicit</u> L2 knowledge that can <u>be used to produce language</u> in real time. **Learning** is the development of the knowledge about <u>L2 rules</u>, which can only be of limited use in helping learners to <u>monitor their language production</u>, but does not help in general with L2 production.

03 Adaptive Control of Thought (ACT) model (by John Anderson) ⓔ

This model concerns skill learning. <u>It proposes that learning progresses from controlled declarative knowledge to automatized procedural knowledge.</u> In this view, <u>declarative knowledge</u> is acquired as separate, self-contained pieces of information. Learning occurs when learners are given new information and are able to verbalize that information. Such information is taught explicitly and the learners (hopefully) can state the knowledge they have gained. On the other hand, <u>procedural knowledge</u> is developed gradually by doing something repeatedly. (**Ex** riding a bike) It can be incomplete or partial, and learners are generally not able to verbalize what they know.

* **Stage 1: Declarative stage** (learned facts do not help learners in actually producing the language.)

* **Stage 2: Associative stage** (learners try to identify patterns in their declarative knowledge so that they can use that knowledge more efficiently for language production. (**Ex**) fewer mistakes, 스스로 feedback, adjustment)

* **Stage 3: Autonomous stage** (learners become more and more automatic in their use of the L2 knowledge through practice.)

04   Additive bilingualism***

context in which the native language is held in prestige by the community or society
For example, children learning English in Montreal, Canada, are proud of their native French language and traditions and therefore can approach the second language more positively, promoting linguistic and cultural diversity.

05   Affective filter hypothesis***

It states that input can only become intake if learners have a low affective filter, that is to say if they view the target language and the learning context favorably. If they have high affective filter, then their resistance towards the language will interfere with their learning.

06   Analyzed language***

the general form in which we know most things with awareness of the structure of that knowledge (see **explicit knowledge**)

07   Anomie***

(완전히 새로운 문화에 동화되지 않은 상태에서) feelings of social uncertainty, dissatisfaction, or homelessness as individuals lose some of the bonds of a native culture

08 Audiolingualism***

(popular in the 1970s and 1980s, behaviourist) primarily focusing on speaking and listening

It viewed language learning as rote learning, repetition, and imitation. It involves learners in mechanical drills where learners repeated numerous sentences and substituted key words. Generally, it was not concerned with the semantic meaning of the sentences and not much emphasis was placed on the relevance of the sentences to the learners.

09 Automatic processes(=processing) / Automaticity***

the ability to retrieve items from long-term memory during language processing without any or with only a very small delay, as opposed to **controlled processes**

It can be developed through practice in language production, such as during interactional speech, or in receptive language use, such as when reading a text.

10 Awareness ⑧

When we are aware of something, we pay conscious attention to it. Schmidt (1995) argued that in order to learn language we have to be aware of it. This has come to be known as the *noticing hypothesis*. Additionally, he argues that the amount of learning that takes place without awareness is minimal. (see also **noticing**)

11 Awareness-raising ⑧

usually, in foreign language classes, calling a learner's attention to linguistic factors that may not otherwise be noticed

12 Backsliding***

a term that refers to learners producing language that is at a lower developmental stage, even though they have progressed to a higher stage

The regression may occur because learners have not fully internalized the current developmental stage.
(in learner language) a phenomenon in which the learner seems to have grasped a rule or principle and then regresses to a previous stage

13　Behaviorism***

It holds that mental process cannot be measured directly, rather they only be inferred from a person's behavior. It sees learning as involving conditioning or the development of a relationship between a stimulus and a response. Education involves the creation and strengthening of these relationships and the speeding up of the connections to the point where they become automatized. Positive reinforcement was believed to encourage specific actions, while negative reinforcement discouraged them.

14　Bilingualism***

relatively equal simultaneous proficiency in two langauges
Compound bilingualism refers to the use of two languages in one context, with one meaning set, while *coordinate bilingualism* refers to using two languages in two separate contexts (Ex home and school), and a presumed separate storage of meanings.

15　Cognition ®

the ability for thinking and processing information
Cognition is a general term to refer to the mental activities and processes that humans engage in.

16　Coherence***

It means the relationship among the meanings expressed in the text. Coherence names the effect of arrangements such that everything in the arrangement gives the appearance of 'naturally' belonging together. It characterizes what appears as an unproblematic state of affairs whether in a social arrangement, or a multimodal sign, text or object. One aspect of coherence is the idea of textual completeness.

17 Cohesion***

Cohesion is the grammatical and lexical linking within a text or sentence that holds a text together and gives it meaning. It is related to the broader concept of coherence. There are two main types of cohesion:

* *Grammatical cohesion*: based on structural content
* **Grammatical cohesive devices such as reference, substitution, ellipsis, and conjunction**

* *Lexical cohesion*: based on lexical content and background knowledge
* **Lexical cohesive devices**: Links are made across a conversation include the use of synonyms, antonyms, repetition of the same content words, words exhibiting general-specific relations, and words displaying part-whole relations. The use of lexical cohesion is an indicator of topic consistency, and hence contributes significantly to the sense that speakers are talking to topic, and the talk, therefore, becomes more coherent.

In Cohesion in English, M.A.K. Halliday and Ruqaiya Hasan identify five general categories of cohesive devices that create coherence in texts: *reference, ellipsis, substitution, lexical cohesion and conjunction.*

* **Reference:** This category involves the relationships between nouns or pronouns and the objects they refer to.
* **Ellipsis:** It occurs when certain words or phrases are omitted in a sentence, but their meaning can be understood from the context.
* **Substitution:** Instead of omitting words, substitution involves replacing a specific word or phrase with a more general one.
* **Lexical cohesion:** This category focuses on the connections between words or phrases based on their lexical or semantic relationships.
* **Conjunctions:** These are words or phrases used to connect words, phrases, or clauses in a sentence, establishing logical relationships between them.

18 Communicative Language Teaching (CLT) ®

an approach to language teaching methodology that emphasizes authenticity, interaction, student-centered learning, task-based activities, and communication of real-world, meaningful purposes

19   Competence [B]

one's underlying knowledge of a system, event, or fact; the unobservable ability to perform language, but not to be confused with **performance**

20   Compound bilingualism***

the use of two languages in one context, with one meaning set

21   Comprehensible input***

It is defined as second language input just beyond the learner's current second language competence, in terms of its syntactic complexity. If a learner's current competence is (i), then comprehensible input is (i+1), the next step in the developmental sequence.

22   Comprehensible output hypothesis***

(in 1985, by Merrill Swain) Swain suggested that not only did learners need comprehensible input for L2 learning, but they also needed to produce comprehensible output. She argued that the learners would benefit from producing the language. When learners actually had to produce the language, they would have to think about what grammatical structures would encode the meanings they were trying to convey. If learners are pushed to produce language that is comprehensible, they will then have to process the language syntactically rather than just semantically. In this way, Swain suggested that output is also a crucial part of the L2 learning process, something that had not been promoted until this point.

23   Comprehension [B]

the process of receiving language; listening or reading; input

24　Conscious learning [Ⓑ]

see **awareness** and **focal attention**

25　Contrastive Analysis Hypothesis (CAH)***

The claim that the principal barrier to second language acquisition is first language interference, and that a scientific analysis of the two languages in question enables the prediction of difficulties a learner will encounter. It assumed that L2 acquisition consists of a transfer of L1 habits to the L2. That is, it suggested that L2 acquisition involved the gradual learning of the differences between the L1 and L2. The greater the differences between structures in the L1 and L2, the more difficult the acquisition of the target language was thought to be. Furthermore, structures in the L1 that were similar to structures in the L2 were more easily transferable by learners.

* **Strong version:** Difficulties in L2 learning could be predicted by differences between the L1 and L2.
* **Weak version:** Contrastive analysis could be useful in explaining some of the linguistic errors that were actually produced by learners.
* Based on research, a difficulty predicted by the CAH is not supported by learners' actual production of the target language. However, it is acknowledge that the characteristics of a learner's first language can influence the learning of a second language, and this has been referred to as **cross-linguistic influence**.

26　Controlled processes / processing***

capacity limited and temporary cognitive efforts, as opposed to **automatic processes**

27　Conversation Analysis (CA)***

a type of analysis that examines talk
CA concerned with how interactional participants use language to do things and to make sense of the interaction. CA is especially interested in turn taking and the repair of communication problems in interaction.

28 Conversational interactions [E]

Conversational interactions are interactions in which two or more people take turns exchanging information and ideas.

29 Coordinate bilingualism***

the use of two languages in two separate contexts (Ex home and school)
This implies that meanings are stored separately for each language.

30 Critical period hypothesis***

The debate about the effects of age on L2 development has resulted in the formation of the critical period hypothesis which states there is a specific age beyond which it is very difficult, if not impossible, for a person to achieve native-speaker-like status in a second language.

31 Cross-linguistic Influence (CLI)***

a concept that replaced the contrastive analysis hypothesis, recognizing the significance of the role of the first language in learning a second, but with an emphasis on the facilitating and interfering effects both languages have on each other

32 Declarative knowledge***

consciously known and verbalizable facts, knowledge and information (in linguistics)

33 Discourse analysis***

(a) the examination of the relationship between forms and functions of language beyond the sentence level
(In reading, **cohesion** and **coherence** are common terms that need to be considered.)
A single sentence can seldom be fully analyzed without considering its context, and since virtually no interactive communication is a single sentence, we string sentences together in interrelated, cohesive stretches of discourse.

(b) a type of analysis that examines the ways in which language is used in interaction
It attempts to describe systematically the talk that occurs in a specific context. Specifically, discourse analysis is often concerned with how specific speech acts such as requests, invitations, complaints, etc., are performed in different contexts.

34 Display question(s)***

an attempt to elicit information already known by the teacher
Lack of authenticity. However, they are not only able to check and test learners, but the source of listening practice for students.

35 Drill***

It is a mechanical technique that focuses on a minimal number of language forms (grammatical or phonological structures) through repetition.

36 Elicitation***

a corrective technique that prompts learner to self-correct (see also **feedback type**)

37   Ellipsis (related to cohesion)***

It happens when, after a more specific mention, <u>words are omitted in the repetition of the phrase.</u>

> **Ex**
>
> * **A simple conversational example**
>   A: Where are you going?
>   B: To dance.
>   The full form of B's reply would be "I am going to dance."
> * **A simple written example**
>   The younger child was very outgoing, the older much more reserved. The omitted words from the second clause are "child" and "was."

38   English as a Foreign Language (EFL) ®

generic term for English learned as a foreign language in a country or context in which English is not commonly used as a language of education, business, or government (**Ex** expanding circle countries)

39   English as a Second Language (ESL) ®

generic term for English learned as a foreign language within the culture of an English-speaking (inner circle) country

40   English as an International Language (EIL) ®

English as a *lingua franca* (공통어) worldwide

41 Error analysis***

the study of leaner errors in the production of L2 speech and writing
Error analysis consists of the *identification, description* and *explanation* of errors. Error analysis identified two types of errors: *interlingual* and *intralingual.* Interlingual *errors* are those that can be attributed to L1 influence. *Intralingual errors* are those that cannot be explained by the L1 and instead are seen as being developmental in nature. Thus, intralingual errors would presumably be made by all learners of the target language, regardless of their L1s.

42 Explicit knowledge***

information that a person knows about language, and usually, the ability to articulate that information (see also **implicit knowledge**)

43 Facilitation***

a type of transfer in which characteristics of the L1 help in the learning of the L2

44 Feedback type***

① explicit correction: an indication to a student that a form is incorrect and providing a corrected form
② recast: an implicit type of corrective feedback that reformulates or expands an ill-formed or incomplete utterance in an unobtrusive way
③ clarification request: an interrogative utterance by which the speaker asks for explanation, confirmation or repetition of an utterance previously produced by the listener, but which has not been perfectly understood (online source)
④ metalinguistic feedback: responses to a learner's output that provide comments, information, or questions related to the linguistics form(s) of the learner's utterance
⑤ elicitation: a corrective technique that prompts the learner to self-correct

⑥ repetition: (in error treatment) in sequential reiteration of an ill-formed part of a student's utterance by a teacher; reiteration by a student of the correct form as a result of teacher feedback, sometimes including incorporation of the correct form in a longer utterance

45 Fossilization***

the relatively <u>permanent incorporation of incorrect linguistic forms</u> into a person's second language competence

46 Grammar consciousness raising***

a concept introduced by Rod Ellis in 1997, <u>the incorporation of forms into communicative tasks</u>
It is closely related to the idea of '**noticing**,' where learners pay attention to specific linguistic features, as opposed to relying on **metalinguistic explanations**. This represents one end of the continuum for FFI.

47 Halliday's seven functions of language (Developmental functions of language)***

According to Halliday, a young child in the early stages of language development is able to master a number of elementary functions of language. Each of these functions has a choice of meanings attached to it. He distinguishes seven initial functions:
① Instrumental ("I want"): used for satisfying material needs
② Regulatory ("do as I tell you"): used for controlling the behaviour of others
③ Interactional ("me and you"): used for getting along with other people
④ Personal ("here I come"): used for identifying and expressing the self
⑤ Heuristic ("tell me why"): used for exploring the world around and inside one
⑥ Imaginative ("Let's pretend"): used for creating a world of one's own
⑦ Informative ("I've got something to tell you"): used for communicating new information

48 Hierarchy of difficulty ®

a teacher or linguist could make a prediction of the relative difficulty of a given aspect of the target language (Stockwell, Bowen, and Martin, 1965). They posited eight possible degrees of difficulty for phonological systems and 16 degrees for grammar. (see also **Contrastive Analysis Hypothesis**)

49 Idiosyncratic dialect***

learner language that emphasizes the notion that a learner's language and the rules that govern it are unique to a particular individual (Corder, 1971)

50 Implicit knowledge***

information that is automatically and spontaneously used in language tasks (see also explicit knowledge)

51 Indicator (Varonis and Gass's (1985) model of negotiation)***

It alerts the speaker of the *trigger* that a problem exists.

52 Input hypothesis***

It states that input that is slightly above a learner's current interlanguage level is necessary for L2 development *(i+1)*. Such input can be made comprehensible by the linguistic and social context. Output, in this view, does not contribute to acquisition.

53 Input***

a term used to describe the language data that are potentially available to the learner
This includes all the visual and auditory language stimuli that surround the learner.
These data could be in the form of authentically occurring language, such as an
overhead conversation or written advertisement, or it could be in the form of
intentionally provided examples of the language in the classroom. In other words, any
example of the language that the learner can potentially perceive is considered input.

54 Intake***

What is actually remembered, subsumed, and internalized from various inputs to the
learner, especially teacher input. It refers to the intermediary stage between input and
acquisition.

55 Integrated approach / skills***

integration of the four skills (listening, reading, speaking and writing)
The four skills are rarely inseparable from the others. It gives students great motivation
that converts to better retention of principles of effective speaking, listening, reading,
and writing.

> **Ex**
> · a pre-reading discussion of a topic to activate schemata, followed by either a reading or
>   a writing task
> · listening to a spoken lecture or monologue, accompanied by note-taking and followed by
>   a discussion

56   Interaction hypothesis***

The claim, by Long, that language competence is the result not only of input, but also of interaction between a learner's input and output. An approach to L2 learning that argues that conversational interaction in the L2 is crucial for learning. The interaction hypothesis proposes that learners receive comprehensible input as they interact with speakers of the L2. One of the ways that input can become comprehensible is through interactional modification (**Cf** negotiation of meaning). The interaction hypothesis also proposes a role for output. As learners produce output, they are able to test their knowledge of the L2 and to receive feedback on their language use. (corrective feedback particularly if the error leads to communication breakdown.)

57   Interface hypothesis***

The issue whether or not explicit L2 knowledge can become implicit L2 knowledge. (To put simplistically, whether or not teaching learners grammatical rules helps them to use the L2 in spontaneous production.)
① non-interface position: Explicit knowledge and implicit knowledge are distinct and that the former has no influence on the latter.
② strong interface position: Explicit knowledge becomes implicit knowledge through practice.
③ weak interface position: It is possible for explicit knowledge to be converted into implicit knowledge and that explicit knowledge can facilitate implicit knowledge by helping learners to notice specific linguistic structures in the input and in their own production. (output)

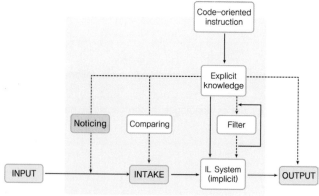

〈Weak interface hypothesis〉, Ellis (2008)

58 Interference^{***}

negative transfer in which <u>a previous item is incorrectly transferred</u> or incorrectly associated with an item to be learned

59 Interlingual transfer^{***}

the effect of one language (usually <u>the first</u>) on another (usually <u>the second</u>)

60 Internalization^{***}

a term from <u>sociocultural theory</u> that refers to the process of learners <u>gaining greater control</u> over the use of the L2

Sociocultural theory argues that learning consists of a progression from *object-regulation* to *other-regulation* to *self-regulation*, in which learners go from <u>relying on external assistance</u> in the performance of activities to being able to <u>perform the activities on their own.</u>

61 Intralingual transfer^{***}

the effect of forms of one language (usually <u>the target language</u>) on other forms <u>with the same language</u> (**Ex** overgeneralization)

62 Language Acquisition Device (LAD) [Ⓔ]

an innate, metaphorical "mechanism" in young children's brains that <u>predisposes them to acquire language</u>

63 Lexical cohesion (related to cohesion)***

Lexical cohesion refers to the way related words are chosen to link elements of a text. There are two forms: *repetition* and *collocation*. Repetition uses the same word, or synonyms, antonyms, etc. For example, "Which dress are you going to wear?" – "I will wear my green frock," uses the synonyms "dress" and "frock" for lexical cohesion. Collocation uses related words that typically go together or tend to repeat the same meaning. An example is the phrase "once upon a time". This is lexical cohesion.

64 Markedness differential hypothesis (=Markedness theory)***

an accounting of relative degrees of difficulty of learning a language by means of principles of universal grammar, also known as markedness theory

① 모국어보다 L2가 유표적(marked)이라면 배우기 어렵다.
　(모국어보다 유표적이지 않은 L2는 더 배우기 쉽다.)
② 학습의 어려움은 L2의 유표성과 비례한다. Degrees of markedness will correspond to degrees of difficulty.

>
>
> *** marked and unmarked**
> · English indefinite articles (*a* and *an*)
> · *an* is the more complex or marked form
> · *a* is the unmarked form with the wider distribution

65 Meaningful learning***

anchoring and relating new items and experiences to knowledge that exists in the cognitive framework (=subsumption, 포섭) (see also **rote learning**)

66   Modified input^{★★★}

interactionally modified input
Learners are not always able to understand the input that is provided for them in conversations. One way in which conversational utterances can be made more comprehensible is when interlocutors negotiate the meanings that they are trying to express. Negotiation might begin when learners signal that they do not understand something that has been said. This signalling may be done through a clarification request or some other indication of non-understanding. Interlocutors may then change their utterances in order to help learners understand the intended meaning. Such interactionally modified input can make the original input comprehensible to learners. It may also help learners to notice the gaps in their interlanguage system, which may help them to learn new linguistic information.

One type of modification is **simplification** (make language less complex by using shorter sentences, simplier grammatical forms or high frequency vocabulary.) Another type of modification is **elaboration** (restating ideas in different ways or repeating segments of the input.) There has been some suggestion that simplified talk may help with learner comprehensible but that it is not helpful for longer-term development. Elaborated talk, on the other hand, has been shown to have a positive effect on acquisition.

Some characteristics of modified input are (1) slower rate, (2) increased use of high frequency vocabulary, (3) simplified syntax (**Ex** short sentences, repetition, fewer clauses), (4) discourse adjustments (**Ex** clear connections between pronouns and their antecedents), and (5) alterations in prosody (**Ex** increased acoustic stress on content words), among others.

67   Modified interaction^{★★★}

By Michael Long who posited an **interaction hypothesis**, redefined comprehensible input and scaffolding as modified interaction
It includes the various modifications that native speakers and other interlocutors create in order to make their input comprehensible to learners.

68 Modified output***

It refers to learner's reformulation of his/her previous utterances and result in a more accurate or complex form in response to an interlocutor's corrective feedback.
Learner production that has been altered in some way, usually in response to a **noticing-of-the-gap**, the realization on the part of the speaker that his or her original utterance was ill-formed in some way or that is was not understood by the recipient. Modified output has been said to be beneficial because it enables the communication to continue and thus increases the amount of exposure to the target language. Producing modified output also helps learners to develop their communicative abilities and stretches them to produce language that is grammatically more complex and accurate than their original utterance.

69 Monitor hypothesis***

It states that learners use their learned knowledge to monitor and, where necessary, self-correct their language production. Learned knowledge never can be the source of spontaneous speech.

70 Motivation ⓑ

Motivation is a psychological construct that refers to the desire and incentive that an individual has to engage in a specific activity. There are different types of motivation that have been proposed and investigated in SLA. One of the earliest distinctions was between *integrative* and *instrumental* motivation. *Integrative motivation* refers to an individual's desire to identify with speakers of the target language. Thus, learners might like the target language culture. In contrast, *instrumental motivation* refers to a need to fulfill some objective. For example, learners may be studying a language because they feel that it will help them get a better job, or because it is a school requirement. It has been argued that integrative motivation generally results in better language learning. Another, slightly different, way in which motivation has been characterized in *intrinsic* and *extrinsic*. *Intrinsic motivation* comes from within an individual. Similar to integrative motivation, it may be the case that the learner likes certain aspects of the target language, its speakers and their culture. *Extrinsic motivation is imposed on the learner by external factors*. For example, a student's parents may require him or her to study a language. Intrinsic motivation is seen as being superior to extrinsic motivation for L2 learning.

71   Multiple intelligences***

the hypothesis that intelligence is not limited to traditional concepts of verbal, logical, and mathematical ability, but has multiple modes including spatial, emotional, musical, contextual, and interpersonal

72   Natural order hypothesis ᴱ

It states that the L2 develops in a specific order, similar to the development of L1 speakers of the language.

73   Negative evidence***

Information about what it is not possible to do linguistically in the target language. Negative evidence could come in the form of corrective feedback or explicit instruction in the target structure.

74   Negative transfer***

This occurs when the learner's L1 knowledge interferes with learning the target language. For example, there may be L1 grammatical rules that the learner tries to apply to the L2, or there may be interference from the L1 lexicon. It may also occur when learners use their L1 phonology when speaking the L2. (see **transfer**)

75 Negotiation of form***

a term coined by Lyster (1998) to contrast with negotiation of meaning
It involves interlocutors paying attention to the incorrect usage of linguistic items during communication, even when no breakdown in communication has occurred. In particular, it refers to the use of prompts to elicit a correction from the learner, rather than providing the correction for the learner in the form of a recast. It is argued that a considerable amount of focus on form constitutes negotiation of form, rather than negotiation of meaning.

76 Negotiation of meaning (=meaning-negotiation strategies)***

Negotiation of meaning is a process that speakers go through to reach a clear understanding of each other. Asking for clarification, rephrasing, and confirming what you think you have understood are all strategies for the negotiation of meaning.

① **comprehension check:** a discourse move that involves a speaker in confirming that an interlocutor has understood the meaning of his or her previous utterance. Comprehension checks may result in the provision of modified input if the interlocutor has not understood the previous meaning.

② **clarification request:** An utterance that tries to elicit from a speaker a revised production that is either linguistically more accurate or semantically more transparent. Clarification requests are a common type of corrective feedback because they indicate that there is a problem with the preceding utterance. Clarification requests are argued to be beneficial for learning because they require learners to produce the correct forms themselves, in contrast to other types of feedback that provide the correct form for the learner.

③ **confirmation check:** A confirmation check is discourse move that involves a speaker verifying the meaning of a previous utterance.

77 Noticing hypothesis***

The noticing hypothesis was proposed by Richard Schmidt to account for the role of attention in L2 learning. Schmidt proposed that learners must attend to linguistic items in the input in order for those forms to have the potential to become intake and eventually a part of the learner's interlangauge system. Thus, noticing requires paying attention with some level of awareness. Schmidt argues that subconscious or implicit learning has a very limited role in L2 acquisition. Rather, learners must first consciously notice a form before it can be learned. According to the noticing hypothesis, nothing is learned unless it has been noticed. Noticing does not itself result in acquisition, but it is the essential starting point. Noticing refers to becoming aware of a language feature in the input.

78 Noticing the gap***

(related to noticing hypothesis) This concept suggest that learners need to discover the difference between their own interlanguage forms and the target language forms. One way to help learners do this is by providing them with corrective feedback when they make L2 production errors. Another way in which learners may notice the gap in their L2 ability is in tasks such as dictogloss, in which learners are asked to reconstruct texts which they have previously heard.

79 Output ®

the language, either written or oral, that is produced by learners
Some theories of SLA, such as universal grammar and Krashen's monitor model view output as merely a result of learning; however, interactionist approaches and sociocultural theory view output as part of the learning process. In fact, Swain proposed the comprehensible output hypothesis to account for the role of output in interactionist approaches to SLA. Regardless of the theoretical approach, one of the functions of output is that it helps learners to practice the L2, thereby developing *fluency* and *automaticity* in the target language.

80 Overgeneralization***

the process of generalizing a particular rule or item in the second language, irrespective of the native language, beyond conventional rules or boundaries
For example, learners may have just learned the present progressive, so they use it frequently, even when it is not appropriate. Another example is when learners apply the English regular past tense to irregular verbs to produce forms such as *eated/ated* or *goed*.

81 Performance ®

the actual production of language by a speaker.

Performance is sometimes distinguished from competence. The latter describes the learners' idealized abstract knowledge of the language. However, in reality, a person's linguistic performance may be less than ideal and may not represent the full extent of the speaker's knowledge. For example, language production may contain mistakes due to situational factors such as distraction or anxiety.

82 Personalization***

When you personalize language, you use it to talk about your knowledge, experience and feelings. Personalization creates better classroom dynamics.

83 Positive evidence***

It consists of examples of what is possible in a language. Thus, all input is potentially evidence to a learner of which linguistic structures and items can occur in the target language. There is agreement among all theories of SLA that positive evidence is necessary for L2 learning; however, there is controversy as to whether it is sufficient for L2 learning, with some researchers arguing that negative evidence is also necessary.

84 Positive transfer***

This occurs when the learner's L1 knowledge facilitates learning the target language. For example, there may be L1 grammatical rules. (see **transfer**)

85   Pragmalinguistics***

(a) the intersection of pragmatics and linguistic forms
(b) the resources for conveying communicative acts and relational or interpersonal meanings, which include pragmatic strategies like <u>directness and indirectness, routines, and a large range of linguistic forms which can intensify or soften communicative acts.</u>
(c) grammatical knowledge, or the **organizational rules** of a language, are fundamental to learning the pragmalinguistic features of an L2

> **Ex**
>
> American teacher: Would you like to read?
> Russian student: No, I would not.
>
> The American teacher used a <u>polite word "would~"</u> as a habit with the Russian student. However, the Russian student received it as a "yes or no" question and answered honestly.

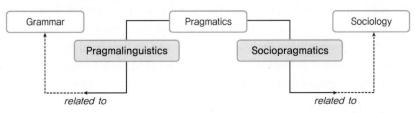

⟨Leech's distinction between pragmalinguistics and sociopragmatics⟩

86   Procedural knowledge***

implicitly known knowledge that is <u>incidentally available but not consciously verbalizable</u>

87   Proficiency ®

a term used to refer to learners' <u>knowledge of and ability to use</u> the target language
Proficiency is often viewed in global terms, that is to say, a learner's <u>overall ability in the L2</u>; however, it may also refer to specific aspects of the language, such as *grammar proficiency* or *pragmatic proficiency*. Additionally, it can be used to refer to the ability to use a specific linguistic feature, such as past tense.

88 Psycholinguistics***

It is concerned with the nature of the processes that the brain undergoes in order to comprehend and produce language. The main focus of psycholinguistics is the search for knowledge and understanding of how humans acquire, generate, and receive language. The main themes in psychololinguistic research are how humans understand spoken and written language, and how we produce and acquire language.

89 Pushed output***

Swain stipulates that for successful SLA, learners should be pushed to produce both written and spoken forms with an emphasis on linguistic accuracy. The term "pushed" means being obliged to perform beyond ones' normal comfort level and "pushed output" refers to the type of output that "reflects what learners can produce when they are pushed to use target language accurately and concisely". Merrill Swain's output hypothesis argues that encouraging learners to produce language that is syntactically slightly more advanced than their actual ability can be beneficial for learning. The utterances that learners produce in such a context is called pushed output. For example, when a learner is encouraged to use a correct verb tense by a teacher's provision of a recast, the learner's response to the correction can be considered pushed output.

90 Reaction to response (Varonis and Gass's (1985) model of negotiation)***

It can tell the speaker of the trigger whether or not the problem has been resolved.

91 Recast***

an implicit type of corrective feedback that formulates or expands an ill-formed or incomplete utterance in an unobstructive way

92   Reference (related to cohesion)***

There are two referential devices that can create cohesion: *Anaphoric reference* occurs when the writer refers back to someone or something that has been previously identified, to avoid repetition. Some examples: replacing "the taxi driver" with the pronoun "he" or "two girls" with "they". Another example can be found in formulaic sequences such as "as stated previously" or "the aforementioned". *Cataphoric reference* is the opposite of anaphora: a reference forward as opposed to backward in the discourse. Something is introduced in the abstract before it is identified. For example: "Here he comes, our award-winning host... it's John Doe!". Cataphoric references can also be found in written text.

93   Referential question(s)***

Request for information not known by the questioner
As in a regular conversation, they lead learners to higher-order thinking, authentic use of language, and longer and more complex answer.

94   Regulation***

a term from sociocultural theory that is used to refer to learning process
Regulation is the ability that individuals have to perform certain tasks. Individuals start out being *object-regulated*, that is to say they use objects to help them perform activities. (**Ex** marbles to learn basic math skills such as addition and subtraction.) Learners progress from object-regulation to other-regulation. *Other-regulation* occurs when other individuals assist in performing a task. The goal of learning process is to become *self-regulated*, whereby individuals have the ability to perform an action on their own.

95 Rehearsal***

(a) an aspect of some definitions of noticing in which linguistic input is repeated in short-term memory. Such rehearsal is said to be an important component of turning intake into learned knowledge.
(b) the act of practicing or repeating an utterance or task before producing it. Rehearsal can take place internally in the learner's mind or it can be done verbally.

96 Repair***

correction by the learner of an ill-formed utterance, either through self-initiated repair, or in response to feedback
(a) (related to Conversation analysis, and Strategic competence) In the case of conversation between second language learners and native speakers, topic clarification often involves seeking or giving repair of linguistic forms that contain errors. It is part of Canale and Swain's (1980) **strategic competence**.
(b) (related to uptake) as a result of teacher feedback, a learner correct an ill-formed utterance, either through **self-repair** or as a result of **peer repair**

97 Repetition***

(a) (in error treatment) the sequential reiteration of an ill-formed part of a student's utterance by a teacher, usually with a change in intonation
(b) (related to social interaction) one of the abilities enabling social interaction, responding to misunderstandings, clarifying, requesting restatements, dealing with interactional "trouble"
(c) (related to uptake) The learner repeats the correct form as a result of teacher feedback, and sometimes incorporates it into a longer utterance.

98 Response (Varonis and Gass's (1985) model of negotiation)***

It is the component through which the speaker of the trigger attemps to resolve the communication difficulty.

99 Rote learning(≒Rote memorizing)***

the process of mentally storing facts, ideas, or feelings having littler or no association with existing cognitive structure (see also **meaningful learning**)

100 Scaffolding***

A concept in sociocultural theory that refers to the help that an expert language user provides to a novice. Scaffolding is the temporary support that surrounds a building under construction. It is interactional support - from teachers, parents, or "better others" - that enables them to perform a task at a level beyond their present competence. The metaphor of scaffolding refers to verbal guidance which an expert provides to help a learner perform any specific task, or the verbal collaboration of peers to perform a task which would be too difficult for any one of them individually.

101 Schematic knowledge (cf. schemata)***

prior knowledge of a topic, used in helping to understand a text

102 Second Language Acquisition (SLA) ®

(a) the process of learning a language other than one's first language
(b) the academic field of investigating how languages other than one's first language are
     learned

103 Self-regulation***

a term from sociocultural theory that represents the goal of the learning process
Sociocultural theory argues that learners go from being other-regulated, meaning that they require assistance from other people or objects in order to complete a specific task, to self-regulated, where they no longer require additional assistance. (as learners become skillful, they need less and less scaffolding and are able to perform the activity without external help.)

104 Silent period***

a period of time in which learners do not produce language
Some researchers argue that (similar to L1 acquisition) L2 learners can go through a stage when they do not, and should not be forced to, produce the L2. However, the fact that learners may not be producing language does not mean that they are not learning. The silent period is optional in L2 learning, and not all learners go through it.

105 Sociocultural Theory (SCT)***

a social theory of learning by Lev Vygotsky, a Russian child psychologist in the 1920s
In the 1990s, SLA researchers began to draw on SCT as a theory of explaning L2 acquisition. SCT views learning as a mediated process in which the individuals develop as they interact with their environment. Such interaction is mediated by tools such as culture and language, which allow individuals to participate in social settings. An important SCT concept for SLA is the *zone of proximal development*. (see also **zone of proximal development, scaffolding**, and **regulation**)

106 Substitution (related to cohesion)***

A word is not omitted, as in ellipsis, but is substituted for another, more general word. For example, "Which ice-cream would you like?" – "I would like the pink one," where "one" is used instead of repeating "ice-cream."

107 Subtractive bilingualism***

contexts in which a target language is held in relatively high esteem while home, native, or heritage languages are devalued
In some regions of the United States, for example, Spanish may be thought to be sociopolitically less desirable than English. A native Spanish-speaking child may feel "ashamed" of Spanish and the child must conquer those feelings along with learning English.

108   Transfer ®

It describes how previous skills or knowledge affect future learning. **Positive transfer** happens when earlier knowledge helps with a new learning task — for example, when a previous item is correctly applied to present subject matter.

It refers to the carryover of previous performance or knowledge to subsequent learning. Positive transfer occurs when the prior knowledge benefits the learning task - that is, when a previous item is correctly applied to present subject matter. **Negative transfer** happens when past skills hinder a new task. The latter can be referred to as **interference** - a previous item is incorrectly transferred or incorrectly associated with an item to be learned.

109   Trigger (Varonis and Gass's (1985) model of negotiation)***

an utterance that causes communication difficulty (utterance or portion of an utterance on the part of the speaker that results in some indication of non-understanding on the part of the hearer)

110   Turn-taking***

It occurs when language production changes from one person to another. The concept is important in interactionist approaches to SLA as well as in *conversation analysis* in which turns are viewed as a basic unit of analysis. It is through turn-taking that interlocutors demonstrate their understanding of the current interaction as they respond to previous turns and produce additional utterances.

111   U-shaped acquisition / development / learning***

the phenomenon of moving from a correct form to an incorrect form and then back to correctness

* **1st stage:** Learners use the irregular past tense correctly.
* **2nd stage:** Learners tend to apply the *-ed* suffix to all verbs. Learners overgeneralize and produce incorrect forms like he *goed*.
* **3rd stage:** Learners learn to distinguish between regular and irregular past tense verbs, and revert to using correct forms like he went.

112 Unanalyzed language***

the general form in which we know most things without being aware of the structure of that knowledge (see **implicit knowledge**)

113 Universal Grammar (UG) ®

a system of linguistic rules that hypothetically apply to all human languages

114 Uptake***

(a) In general terms, it can refer to what learners learn or report having learned. One way that this type of uptake has been measured is by giving learners uptake charts at the end of a lesson and asking them to write down everything they remember learning from the lesson.

(b) a student utterance that immediately follows a teacher's feedback and that constitutes a reaction in some way to the teacher's intention to draw attention to some aspect of the student's initial utterance. It is considered successful when learners repair their initially incorrect utterance; however, uptake may be unsuccessful if learners fail to repair (*needs repair*) their original error. Some argued that as a type of pushed output, uptake benefits learners because it encourages them to stretch their interlangauge system. In addition, uptake has been argued to be an indication of noticing; however, it is acknowledged that the absence of uptake does not necessarily indicate a lack of.

> **Ex**
>
> L: I will be *studied* in school for two years to get degree.
> T: Really? Someone will *study* you?
> L: Oh! No, I must *study* for two years, at UCLA, for degree in MBA.

115   Whole language education***

an emphasis on the interconnections between oral and written language and the integration of all four skills
The model offered three important insights:
(a) Language is not the sum of its many dissectible and discrete parts.
(b) Integrate the four skills (listening, speaking, reading, and writing)
(c) Language is a system of social practices that both constrain and liberate.

116   Zone of Proximal Development (ZPD)***

the distance between a learner's existing developmental state and his or her potential development
In SLA theory, the relationship between the novice learner and expert teacher is also viewed as important in enabling the learner to do more on his or her own. However, SLA theory has also shown that learners can assist each other in the ZPD, with the result that they may be able to produce language together that is more advanced than either one could produce individually.

※ **Read the following descriptions and fill in the blanks.**

01 _____ _____ **hypothesis**

It states that <u>input can only become intake</u> if learners have a <u>low filter</u>, that is to say if they view the target language and the learning context favorably. If they have <u>high filter</u>, then their resistance towards the language will <u>interfere with their learning</u>.

02 _____

feelings of <u>social uncertainty</u>, dissatisfaction, or <u>homelessness</u> as individuals lose some of the bonds of a native culture

03 _____

(popular in the 1970s and 1980s, behaviourist) primarily focusing on <u>speaking and listening</u>
It viewed language learning as <u>rote learning, repetition, and imitation</u>. It involves learners in <u>mechanical drills</u> where learners repeated numerous sentences and substituted key words. Generally, it was not concerned with the semantic meaning of the sentences and not much emphasis was placed on the relevance of the sentences to the learners.

04 _____ **processes**

the ability to retrieve items from <u>long-term memory</u> during language processing without any or with only a very small delay, as opposed to **controlled processes**
It can be developed <u>through practice in language production</u>, such as during interactional speech, or in receptive language use, such as when reading a text.

05 _____

a term that refers to learners producing language that is at a lower developmental stage, even though they have progressed to a higher stage

The regression may occur because learners have not fully internalized the current developmental stage.

(in learner language) a phenomenon in which the learner seems to have grasped a rule or principle and then regresses to a previous stage

06 _____   _____

It is defined as second language input just beyond the learner's current second language competence, in terms of its syntactic complexity. If a learner's current competence is (i), then THIS is (i+1), the next step in the developmental sequence.

07 _____

It is a mechanical technique that focuses on a minimal number of language forms (grammatical or phonological structures) through repetition.

08 _____

the relatively permanent incorporation of incorrect linguistic forms into a person's second language competence; also referred to as stabilization

09 _____ **hypothesis**

The claim, by Long, that <u>language competence</u> is the result not only of input, but also of <u>interaction between a learner's input and output</u>. An approach to L2 learning that argues that conversational interaction in the L2 is crucial for learning. THIS proposes that learners receive comprehensible input as they interact with speakers of the L2. One of the ways that input can become comprehensible is <u>through interactional modification</u> (**Cf** <u>negotiation of meaning</u>). THIS also proposes a role for output. As learners produce output, they are able to <u>test their knowledge</u> of the L2 and to receive feedback on their language use. (<u>corrective feedback</u> particularly if the error leads to communication breakdown.)

10 _____

negative transfer in which <u>a previous item is incorrectly transferred</u> or incorrectly associated with an item to be learned

11 _____ _____

the effect of one language (usually <u>the first</u>) on another (usually <u>the second</u>)

12 _____ _____

the effect of forms of one language (usually <u>the target language</u>) on other forms with the <u>same language</u> (**Ex** overgeneralization)

13 _____ _____

anchoring and relating <u>new items and experiences to knowledge that exists</u> in the cognitive framework (=subsumption)

14 _____ _____

By Michael Long who posited an **interaction hypothesis**, redefined <u>comprehensible input</u> and <u>scaffolding</u> as modified interaction
It includes the various modifications that native speakers and other interlocutors create in order to make their input comprehensible to learners.

15 _____ **hypothesis**

It states that learners use their <u>learned knowledge to monitor</u> and, where necessary, self-correct their language production. Learned knowledge can never be the source of spontaneous speech.

16 _____ **hypothesis**

According to THIS hypothesis, nothing is learned unless it has been noticed. THIS does not itself result in acquisition, but it is the essential starting point. THIS refers to becoming aware of a language feature in the input.

17 _____

When you personalize language, you use it to talk about your <u>knowledge, experience and feelings</u>. THIS creates better classroom dynamics.

18 _____ **question(s)**

Request for information not known by the questioner
As in a regular conversation, they lead learners to higher-order thinking, authentic use of language, and longer and more complex answer.

19 _____ _____

the process of mentally storing facts, ideas, or feelings having littler or no association with existing cognitive structure (see also **meaningful learning**)

20 _____

A concept in sociocultural theory that refers to the help that an expert language user provides to a novice. THIS is the temporary support that surrounds a building under construction. It is interactional support - from teachers, parents, or "better others" - that enables them to perform a task at a level beyond their present competence. The metaphor of THIS refers to verbal guidance which an expert provides to help a learner perform any specific task, or the verbal collaboration of peers to perform a task which would be too difficult for any one of them individually.

21 _____ _____ **(cf. _____)**

prior knowledge of a topic, used in helping to understand a text

22 _____ _____

a period of time in which learners do not produce language
Some researchers argue that (similar to L1 acquisition) L2 learners can go through a stage when they do not, and should not be forced to, produce the L2. However, the fact that learners may not be producing language does not mean that they are not learning. THIS is optional in L2 learning, and not all learners go through it.

23 _____ **acquisition / development / learning**

the phenomenon of <u>moving from a correct form to an incorrect form and then back to correctness</u> (1st stage: Learners use the irregular past tense correctly, 2nd: Learners tend to apply the -ed suffix to all verbs. Learners overgeneralize and produce incorrect forms like he goed, 3rd: Learners learn to distinguish between regular and irregular past tense verbs, and revert to using correct forms like he went.)

24 _____

<u>a student utterance that immediately follows a teacher's feedback</u> and that constitutes a reaction in some way to the teacher's intention to draw attention to some aspect of the student's initial utterance.

25 _____ _____ _____ _____

the distance between a learner's <u>existing developmental state and his or her potential development</u>
In SLA theory, the relationship between the novice learner and expert teacher is also viewed as important in enabling the learner to do more on his or her own. However, SLA theory has also shown that learners can assist each other in THIS, with the result that they may be able to produce language together that is more advanced than either one could produce individually.

Answers

01 Affective filter

02 Anomie

03 Audiolingulalism

04 Automatic

05 Backsliding

06 Comprehensible input

07 Drill

08 Fossilization

09 Interaction hypothesis

10 Interference

11 Interlingual transfer

12 Intralingual transfer

13 Meaningful learning

14 Modified interaction

15 Monitor

16 Noticing

17 Personalization

18 Referential

19 Rote learning

20 Scaffolding

21 Schematic knowledge (cf. schemata)

22 Silent period

23 U-shaped

24 Uptake

25 Zone of proximal development

Note

Learner-related Terms

(Learning Strategies, Styles, Variables & Interlanguage)

※ **Review the following Key Terms list and put a checkmark next to Terms that you do not know the exact meaning.**

☐　Affective domain

☐　Affective factors

☐　Affective filter

☐　Affective strategy

☐　Agency

☐　Ambiguity intolerance

☐　Ambiguity tolerance (tolerance of ambiguity)

☐　Amotivation

☐　Analytic learning style

☐　Anxiety

☐　Auditory learning style

☐　Avoidance

☐　Basic Interpersonal Communication Skills (BICS)

☐　Cognitive strategies

☐　Cognitive style

☐　Collaboration

☐　Communication strategies

☐　Compensatory strategies (communication strategies)
　　① avoidance　② circumlocution　③ approximation　④ word coinage
　　⑤ prefabricated patterns　⑥ code-switching　⑦ appeal to authority　⑧ literal translation
　　⑨ keeping the floor　⑩ foreignizing　⑪ nonlinguistic signals

☐　Contrastive analysis

☐　Covert error(s)

☐　Debilitative anxiety

☐　Demotivation

☐　Difficulty

- [ ] Emergent stage
- [ ] Emotional intelligence (EQ, Emotional Quotient)
- [ ] Empathy
- [ ] Equilibration
- [ ] Errors of addition, omission, substitution, and permutation
- [ ] Extent
- [ ] Extrinsic motivation
- [ ] Extroversion
- [ ] Facilitative anxiety
- [ ] Field Dependence (FD)
- [ ] Field Independence (FI)
- [ ] Field sensitivity
- [ ] Global error(s)
- [ ] Global self-esteem
- [ ] High Input Generators (HIGs)
- [ ] Hypercorrection
- [ ] Identity
- [ ] Impulsivity (impulsive style)
- [ ] Induced error(s)
- [ ] Inhibition
- [ ] Instrumental orientation
- [ ] Integrative orientation
- [ ] Interactional competence
- [ ] Intercultural competence
- [ ] Interlanguage (4 developmental stages) ① pre-systematic stage ② emergent stage ③ systematic stage ④ stabilization stage
- [ ] Interlingual transfer
- [ ] Intralingual transfer
- [ ] Intrinsic motivation

- [ ] Introversion
- [ ] Kinesthetic learning style
- [ ] Language anxiety
- [ ] Language ego
- [ ] Learnability
- [ ] Learner language
- [ ] Learning strategies
- [ ] Learning style
- [ ] Left-brain dominance
- [ ] Local error(s)
- [ ] Low Input Generators (LIGs)
- [ ] Metacognitive strategy(ies)
- [ ] Motivation
- [ ] Orientation
- [ ] Overt error(s)
- [ ] Peer pressure
- [ ] Postsystematic stage
- [ ] Prefabricated patterns
- [ ] Presystematic (error)
- [ ] Proactive inhibition
- [ ] Rapport
- [ ] Reflectivity (reflective style)
- [ ] Retroactive inhibition
- [ ] Right-brain dominance
- [ ] Risk taking
- [ ] Second identity
- [ ] Self-actualization
- [ ] Self-correction

- [ ] Self-determination
- [ ] Self-efficacy
- [ ] Self-esteem
- [ ] Self-regulation
- [ ] Situation self-esteem
- [ ] Socioaffective strategies
- [ ] Sociocultural-Interactive (S-I) strategy
- [ ] Sociolinguistic competence
- [ ] Stabilization
- [ ] State anxiety
- [ ] Strategic competence
- [ ] Strategic self-regulation (S²R)
- [ ] Strategy
- [ ] Styles
- [ ] Systematicity
- [ ] Task self-esteem
- [ ] Tolerance of ambiguity
- [ ] Trait anxiety
- [ ] Variation
- [ ] Visual,
      auditory,
      tactile,
      kinesthetic learning styles
- [ ] Willingness To Communicate (WTC)
- [ ] Working memory

01   Affective domain ⓑ

emotional issues and factors in human behavior, often compared to the cognitive domain

02   Affective factors ⓑ

self-esteem, self-efficacy, willingness to communicate, inhibition, risk-taking, anxiety, emphathy, extrovert, introvert

03   Affective filter (by Stephan Krashen)***

a metaphorical construct that accounts for how learners' internal emotional state may influence their learning
When the affective filter is high (when learners feel negatively about the L2 or the L2 learning process), the filter will prevent input from becoming intake. On the other hand, if the affective filter is low, learners are more easily able to incorporate the input around them into their interlanguage system.

04   Affective strategy(ies)***

one of three categories of metastrategy, strategies and tactics that help the learner to employ beneficial emotional energy, form positive attitudes toward learning, and generate motivation

05   Agency***

a person's ability to make choices, take control, self regulate, and thereby pursue goals as an individual, leading potentially to personal or social transformation

06   Ambiguity intolerance***

a style in which an individual is relatively ill-equipped to withstand or manage a high degree of uncertainty in a linguistic context, and as a result may demand more certainty and structure

07   Ambiguity tolerance (tolerance of ambiguity) ↔ Ambiguity intolerance***

a style in which an individual is relatively well suited to withstand or manage a high degree of uncertainty in a linguistic context

08   Amotivation***

the absence of any motivation entirely

09   Analytic learning style Ⓔ

Analytic learners are easily able to identify patterns in the L2 input and to analyze language into its various components.

* **Deductively:** When learners are presented with metalinguistic rules to help them examine L2 input.
* **Inductively:** When learners extract rules of the language by identifying systematic patterns in the input.

Analytic learners may benefit more from explicit language instruction, but this advantage does not seem to extend to more meaning-focused types of instruction.

10 Anxiety***

the subjective feeling of tension, apprehension, and nervousness connected to an arousal of the autonomic nervous system, and associated with feelings of uneasiness, frustration, self-doubt, apprehension or worries (facilitative anxiety, and debilitative anxiety)

11 Auditory learning style***

the tendency to prefer listening to lectures and audiotapes, as opposed to visual and/or kinesthetic processing

12 Avoidance***

Learners may choose not to use certain L2 structures(topic, voca, grammar) if those structures are difficult or problematic to them. Instead they may use language that is simpler and easier for them to produce. Avoidance may therefore result in language that is more accurate or fluent, but the language may be less complex or advanced. (see also **communication strategeis**)

(a) (of a topic) in a conversation, steering others away from an unwanted topic
(b) (of a language form) a strategy that leads to refraining from producing a form that speaker may not know, often through an alternative form

as a strategy, options intended to prevent the production of ill-formed utterances, classified into such categories as syntactic, lexical, phonological, and topic avoidance

13 Basic Interpersonal Communication Skills (BICS) Ⓔ

abilities that enable language users to function in everyday personal exchanges; context-embedded performance (Compared to Cognitive Academic Language Proficiency (CALP))

> **Ex**
> informal / friendly exchages / slang, metaphor

14 Cognitive strategies***

strategic options <u>relating to specific learning tasks</u> that involve direct manipulation of the learning material itself - *activating knowledge, contextualization, predicting, guessing, inferencing, skimming, scanning*

15 Cognitive style***

the way a person learns material or solve problems, cognitive domain which contributes to individual differences

16 Collaboration***

the process of learners <u>working together</u> (as opposed to individually) with their classmates in reaching goals of a task, solving problems, practicing language, etc.

17 Communication strategies (Dörnyei,1995)***

(a) strategic options relating to output, how one productively expresses meaning, and how one effectively delivers messages to others, as opposed to **learning strategies**
(b) What others call **sociocultural-interactive (S-I)** strategies (Oxford, 2011b), or **socioaffective strategies** (O'Malley et all., 1985b)

18 Compensatory strategies (communication strategies)***

① avoidance: avoiding a topic, concept, grammatical construction, or phonological element that poses difficulty
② circumlocution: describing an object or idea with a definition

③ approximation: using an alternative term which expresses the meaning of the target lexical item as closely as possible

④ word coinage: creating a nonexistent L2 word based on a supposed rule

⑤ prefabricated patterns: using memorized stock phrases, usually for "survival" purposes

⑥ code-switching: using an L1 word with L1 pronunciation while speaking in L2

⑦ appeal to authority: asking for aid either directly or indirectly (usually direct appeal)

⑧ literal translation: translating a lexical item, an idiom, or a structure from the learners' L1 to L2

⑨ keeping the floor: using fillers or hesitation devices to fill pauses and to gain time to think. (well, now let's see, uh, as a matter of fact)

⑩ foreignizing: using an L1 word by adjusting it to L2 phonology and/or morphologically (Ex adding it to a L2 suffix)

⑪ nonlinguistic signals: mime, gesture, facial expression, or sound imitation

19 Contrastive analysis***

the comparative study of two or more languages to identify similarities and differences between their grammatical, phonological, lexical and pragmatic systems. In the 1960s, contrastive analysis served as a basis for the *contrastive analysis hypothesis* which claimed that the greater differences between structures in the L1 and L2, the more difficult the acquisition of the L2.

20 Covert error(s)***

errors that are grammatically well formed at the sentence level but not interpretable within the context of communication; discourse errors. Covert errors only become apparent when a larger stretch of discourse is considered, rather than only inspecting the sentence. (see also **overt errors**)

>
> We're here for three weeks.
> meaning: We're staying here for three weeks in total.
> 화자의 의도: We've been here for three weeks.

21　Debilitative anxiety[***]

Debilitative anxiety <u>views stressors as threats and interferes</u> with performance. It is the level of anxiety which is perceived as threatening. A study implied that perceiving anxiety as debilitative is associated with emotional exhaustion. A similar study found out that students who experienced debilitating test anxiety had lower average class scores for the semester.

22　Demotivation[***]

losing interest and drive that once was present

23　Difficulty[***]

the extent to which <u>language or an activity involving language is challenging</u> for the learner
Thus, it is a <u>subjective term</u> as different aspects of the language and different activities may be more or less difficult for each individual learner. Also, difficulty related to both *ability* and *affect*. For example, a stressful situation such as <u>public speaking may raise anxiety</u> and in turn make language production <u>more difficult than in pair-work activity</u> in class. Difficulty could be said to be the subjective experience of complexity.

24　Emergent stage[***]

(of learner language) one in which the learner <u>grows in consistency</u> in linguistic production

25　Emotional intelligence (EQ, Emotional Quotient)[***]

associated with Goleman, a mode of intelligence that places emotion, and/or the management of emotions, at the seat of intellectual functioning

26 Empathy***

"putting yourself into someone else's shoes," reaching beyond the self to understand what another person is thinking or feeling

27 Equilibration***

progressive interior organization of knowledge in a stepwise fashion; moving from states of doubt and uncertainty (disequilibrium) to stages of resolution and certainty (equilibrium)

28 Errors of addition, omission, substitution, and permutation***

a classification of error in terms of standard mathematical categories. These categories help a teacher to pinpoint an error in order to ascertain potential treatment.

> **Ex**
> (a) Why to not form worse make a little better? (added *to* infinitive)
> (b) I went to movie. (omitted definite article, *the*)
> (c) I lost my road. (the word road is substituted for *way*)
> (d) She have will been here two years next month. (permuted auxiliaries, *will have*)

29 Extent ®

the rank of linguistic unit that would have to be deleted, replaced, supplied, or reordered in order to repair the sentence (Lennon, 1991)

> **Ex**
> I was so depressed. However, I felt the world was coming to end.
> : This sentence has a discourse error in that the connector *however* does not fit the rest of the second sentence. The extent would be either to change the whole second clause to a positive connotation or simply change the connector to something like *also*.

30   Extrinsic motivation***

a motivational orientation to language learning that comes from a source external to the learner (Ex studying a language in order to complete a school requirement or to get a job promotion)

31   Extroversion***

the extent to which a person has a deep-seated need to receive ego enhancement, self-esteem, and a sense of wholeness from other people, as opposed to receiving that affirmation within oneself

32   Facilitative anxiety***

Facilitative anxiety views stressors as challenges and assists performance. It is the level of anxiety which is perceived as motivating. People with this kind of anxiety interpret stressors as challenges instead of threats. For instance, perceiving anxiety as facilitative has been found out to be positively associated with academic performance and negatively associated with emotional exhaustion.

33   Field Dependence (FD)***

the tendency to be "dependent" on the total field so that the parts embedded in the filed are not easily perceived, although that total field is perceived more clearly as a unified whole (=field sensitivity) (Ex global learners)

34   Field Independence (FI)***

ability to perceive a particular, relevant item or factor in a "field" of distracting items (Ex analytic learner)

35 Field sensitivity***

the same as field dependence, with an emphasis on the positive aspects of the style (see also **field dependence**)

36 Global error(s)***

errors that <u>hinder communication</u> or prevent a hearer (or reader) from comprehending some aspect of a message (**Ex** word order)

37 Global self-esteem***

self-esteem in overall (see also **self-esteem**)
It's how someone generally judges their own value over time and in different situations.

38 High Input Generators (HIGs)***

people who are adept at initiating and sustaining interaction, or "generating" input from <u>teachers, peers, and other speakers</u> of the language in an arena, as opposed to *low input generators*

39 Hypercorrection***

a phenomenon in which language <u>speakers overuses language rules in contexts</u> where they do not apply
A speaker or writer who produces a hypercorrection generally believes through a misunderstanding of such rules that the form is more "correct", standard, or otherwise preferable, <u>often combined with a desire to appear formal or educated</u>. For example,

the correction of the subject-positioned "you and me" to "you and I" leads people to "internalize the rule that 'you and I' is somehow more proper, and they end up using it in places where they should not – such as 'he gave it to you and I' when it should be 'he gave it to you and me.'" Often, the linguistic form being overused in seen as being socially more prestigious. (see also **overgenerlization**)

02

40   Identity***

the extent to which L2 learners do not perceive themselves merely as individual entities, but more importantly, as an integral and constitutive part of the social world to which they are connected

41   Impulsivity (impulsive style)***

an individual's tendency to be comfortable making quick or gambling decisions
Taking linguistic risks in the face of possible error. Taking initiative in conversations. (see also **reflectivity**)

42   Induced error(s)***

errors caused by something in the learner's environment, such as the teacher, a textbook, or the classroom methodology

43   Inhibition***

apprehension over one's self-identity or fear of showing self-doubt, leading to building mechanisms of protective self-defense

44 Instrumental orientation***

acquiring a language as a means for attaining instrumental goals, such as acquiring a degree or certificate in an academic institution, furthering a career, reading technical material, translation, etc.

45 Integrative orientation***

learning a language in order to integrate oneself into the culture of a second language group and become involved in social interchange in that group

46 Interactional competence***

the ability to interact communicatively with a focus on such interactional factors as participant identity, construction of interpersonal meanings, turn-taking and sociopragmatics

47 Intercultural competence***

ability to understand, empathize with, and/or function in a culture or cultures other than one's L1 culture
While much of our attention as teachers in SLA classrooms is focused on communicative competence, we must also be mindful of the place of intercultural competence. Intercultural competence involves understanding and navigating complex cultural interactions where the rules and norms are not easily negotiated. It includes the exchange of values and identities across different cultures, and the ability to recognize and adapt to shifts and new interpretations of meaning that arise during these exchanges.

48 Interlanguage***

learner language that emphasizes the separateness of a second language learner's system, a system that has a structurally intermediate status between the native and target languages. The language system that is created by L2 learners as they develop their L2 knowledge towards the target language norms. A learners' interlanguage is systematic and rule-governed, even though the system may differ from the target language grammar. Interlanguage systems do not remain static; they are dynamic and develop as learners continue to receive input and to restructure their L2 knowledge. Instead of viewing errors as something to avoid, interlanguage theory recognizes that the 'mistakes' that learners make are to be expected as part of the learning process. (4 developmental stages: pre-systematic stage, emergent stage, systematic stage, stabilization stage)

49 Interlingual transfer***

the effect of one language on another

50 Intralingual transfer***

the effect of forms, patterns, and discourse conventions of one language (usually the L2) on other forms, patterns, and discourse conventions within the same language

51 Intrinsic motivation***

This type of motivation is internal to the learner. It is characterized by positive feelings towards the language, its speakers and their culture. (**Ex**) studying Japanese because a person likes anime and manga; learning a language because a person enjoys the challenge of analysing a language) For a time it was thought intrinsic motivation was superior to extrinsic motivation; however there is no conclusive evidence that this is always the case. Also, the distinction between the two types of motivation is not always clear. Intrinsic motivation is similar to integrative motivation, a term introduced by Gardner and Lambert. (1972)

52 Introversion***

the extent to which a person derives a sense of wholeness and fulfillment from within, apart from a reflection of this self from other people

53　Kinesthetic learning style***

the tendency to prefer demonstrations and physical activity involving bodily movement

54　Language anxiety***

a feeling of worry experienced in relation to a foreign language, either trait or state in nature

Recent research on language anxiety focuses more specifically *on the situational nature of state anxiety*.

① 외국어를 이용한 의사소통에 대한 불안: communication apprehension, arising from learners' inability to adequately express mature thoughts and ideas

② 타인에게 긍정적인 인상을 남기고자 하는 마음에서 발생하는 불안: fear of negative social evaluation, arising from a learner's need to make a positive social impression on others

③ 학업적으로 평가받는 것에 대한 불안: test anxiety, or apprehension over academic evaluation

(see also **anxiety**)

55　Language ego***

the identity a person develops in reference to the language he or she speaks

56　Learnability***

the relative difficulty of acquiring a linguistic item, depending on the learners' developmental readiness or developmental stage (psycholinguistically "ready")

The concept of learnability is based on studies which have found that the acquisition of syntactic structures and morphemes often occurs in a fixed order. Linguistic items that are several stages beyond the learner's current level have low learnability. Thus, learnability is not an inherent quality of a specific structure, since the learnability of an item cannot be measured independently from the learner's level.

57 Learner language [B]

generic term used to describe a learner's interlanguage or interlanguage system

58 Learning strategies***

strategic options relating to input, processing, storage, and retrieval, or taking in messages from others, as opposed to **communication strategies**

59 Learning style***

cognitive, affective, and physiological traits that are relatively stable indicators of how learners perceive, interact with, and respond to the learning environment

60 Left-brain dominance***

a style that favors logical, analytical thought, with mathematical and linear processing of information

61 Local error(s)***

errors that do not prevent a message from being understood, usually due to a minor violation of one segment of a sentence, allowing the hearer/reader to make an accurate guess about the intended meaning

62 Low Input Generators (LIGs)***

relatively passive learners who do little to create opportunities for input to be directed toward them, as opposed to High Input Generators

63   Metacognitive strategy(ies)***

strategic options that relate to one's "executive" functions; strategies that involve planning for learning, thinking about the learning process as it is taking place, monitoring of one's production or comprehension, and evaluating learning after an activity is completed. - *planning, organizing, monitoring, evaluating*

64   Motivation ®

the anticipation of reward, whether *internally* or *externally* administered; choices made about goals to pursue and the effort exerted in their completion (≒ students' attitudes)

65   Orientation***

one's personal perspective on a culture other than one's own, and the extent to which that perspective influences the intensity of motivation to understand or adapt to that culture and/or the language of the culture (≒ students' main purpose)
An *instrumental orientation* referred to acquiring a language as a means for attaining practical goals such as furthering a career, reading technical material, or translation. An *integrative orientation* described learners who wished to integrate themselves into the culture of the second language group and become involved in social interchange in that group. Some researchers argued that instrumentality and integrativeness are not actually types of motivation, but rather, more appropriately forms of orientations. That is, depending on whether a learner's main focus or purpose is (1) academic or career related (instrumental), or (2) socially or culturally oriented (integrative), different needs might be fulfilled in learning an L2.

66   Overt error(s)***

errors that are unquestionaly ungrammatical at the sentence level
Overt errors can be detected by inspecting the sentence or utterance in which it occurs. (see also **covert errors**)

67   Peer pressure***

encouragement, often among children, to conform to the behavior, attitudes, language, etc., of those around them

68   Postsystematic stage***

a stage in which the learner has relatively few errors and has mastered the system to the point that fluency and intended meanings are not problematic; stabilization

69   Prefabricated patterns***

memorized chunks of language - words, phrases, short sentences - the component parts of which the speaker is unaware

70   Presystematic (error)***

an error in which the learner is only vaguely aware that there is some systematic order to a particular class of items; random error

71   Proactive inhibition***

failure to retain rote material because of interfering effects of similar material learned before the learning task, as opposed to **retroactive inhibition**
Since rotely learned material is not substantively merged into cognitive structure, its retention is influenced primarily by the interfering effects of similar rote material learned immediately before or after the learning task.

72   Rapport***

(a) the relationship or connection a teacher establish with students
(b) a relationship built on trust and respect that leads to students' feeling capable, competent, and creative

> **Ex**
>
> *** Strategies for establishing rapport**
> · Show interest in each student as a person.
> · Give feedback on each person's progress.
> · Openly solicit students' ideas and feelings.
> · Value and respect what students think and say.
> · Laugh with them and not at them.
> · Work with them as a team, not against them.
> · Develop a genuine sense of vicarious joy when they learn something or otherwise succeed.

73   Reflectivity (reflective style)***

an individual's tendency to make slower, more calculated decisions
Taking time to mentally sort through linguistic complexity. Speaking out only when certain of linguistic systems. (see also **impulsivity**)

74   Retroactive inhibition***

failure to retain material because of interfering effects of similar material learned after the learning task, as opposed to **proactive inhibition**
Since rotely learned material is not substantively merged into cognitive structure, its retention is influenced primarily by the interring effects of similar rote material learned immediately before or after the learning task.

75　Right-brain dominance***

a style in which one favors visual, tactile, and auditory images and is more efficient in processing holistic, integrative, and emotional information

76　Risk taking***

willingness to gamble, to try out hunches about a language with the possibility of being wrong

77　Second identity***

an alternate ego, different from one's first language ego, that develops in reference to a second language and/or culture (see **language ego**)

78　Self-actualization***

reaching the pinnacle of one's potential; the culmination of human attainment

79　Self-correction***

This occurs when learners repair their own incorrect language production. Self-correction can be the result of learners *monitoring* - that is paying attention to - their own output. Self-correction may be one way in which explicit L2 knowledge can be used to help learners produce accurate language while they are speaking.

80　Self-determination***

one's own choice to make an effort because of what he or she will gain, either in the short term or long run

81 Self-efficacy***

belief in one's own capabilities to perform a specific activity

82 Self-esteem***

self-appraisal, self-confidence, knowledge of oneself, usually categorized into "global" (overall), "situational/specific" (in a general context), and "task" (particular activities within a context)

83 Self-regulation***

(a) deliberate, self-stimulated, goal-directed management, control, and application of cognitive, affective, and sociocultural-interactive strategies to aid in learning a foreign language
(b) the autonomous process of developing awareness, setting goals, monitoring performance, using effective strategies, and holding positive beliefs about oneself

84 Situation self-esteem***

self-esteem in particular life contexts, such as work, education, play, home, or in certain relatively discretely defined skills, such as communicative, athletic, musical, or mathematical ability (see also **self-esteem**)

85 Socioaffective strategies***

strategies that help learners regulate and control emotions, motivations, and attitudes towards learning, as well as help learners learn through contact and interaction with others (strategic options relating to social-mediating activity and interacting with others)

86 Sociocultural-interactive (S-I) strategy***

one of three categories of metastrategy, strategies and tactics that help the learner to interact and communicate, to compensate for knowledge gaps, and to deal effectively with culture

87 Sociolinguistic competence (≒ sociocultural competence)***

ability to use or apply sociocultural rules of discourse in a language

88 Stabilization***

a concept that refers to the fact that a learner's interlanguage system may cease develop before it achieves target-like accuracy
However, unlike *fossilization*, stabilization does not imply that a learner's knowledge of a specific structure cannot develop further, but rather it implies that there is no further learning at the moment. It is typically used to refer to specific linguistic structures, rather than to the learners interlanguage system as a whole. Stabilization acknowledges that as long as a learner is alive, there may be the possibilities for further L2 development. (see also **postsystematic stage**, and **fossilization**)

89 State anxiety***

a relatively temporary feeling of worry experienced in relation to some particular event or act, as opposed to trait anxiety

90 Strategic competence***

(according to Canale & Swain) the ability to use strategies to compensate for imperfect knoweldge of rules or performance limitations; (according to Bachman) the ability to assess a communicative context and plan and execute production responses to accomplish intended purposes

91 Strategic self-regulation (S²R)***

the self-simulated application by a learner of cognitive, affective, and sociocultural-interactive strategies (Oxford, 2011b)

S²R model is the principle of learners acting on their learning. Autonomy and awareness without action would be relatively useless. Once learners can become aware of their predispositions, their styles, and their strengths and weaknesses, they can then take appropriate action in the form of a plethora of self-regulated strategies that are available to them. Not all strategies are appropriate for all learners.

According to Oxford, strategically self-regulated learners do the following:
* Actively participate in their own autonomous learning process.
* Control various aspects of their learning for accomplishing specific goals.
* Regulate their cognitive and affective states.
* Form positive beliefs about themselves.
* Use strategies to move from conscious knowledge to automatic procedural knowledge.
* Select appropriate strategies for widely differing purposes and contexts.
* Make the connection between strategy use and learning outcomes.

92 Strategy ®

any number of specific methods or techniques for approaching a problem or task; modes of operation for achieving a particular end; planned designs for controlling and manipulating certain information; a type of activity that learners are involved in to help them in L2 learning, L2 production or L2 comprehension.

93 Styles ®

consistent and enduring tendencies or preferences within an individual; general characteristics of intellectual and emotional functioning that differentiate one person from another

94 Systematicity***

consistency and predictability in learner language

95 Task self-esteem***

self-esteem related to particular tasks within specific situations. Within the educational domain, task self-esteem might refer to one subject-matter area. (see also **self-esteem**)

96 Tolerance of ambiguity***

ambiguity tolerance

97 Trait anxiety***

a relatively permanent predisposition to be anxious about a number of things, as opposed to *state anxiety*

98 Variation(=variability)***

instability in learners' linguistic system (interlanguage)

99 Visual, auditory, tactile, kinesthetic learning styles***

- Visual learners tend to prefer reading and studying charts, drawings, and other graphic information.
- Auditory learners prefer listening to lectures and audiotapes.
- Tactile learner is a "hands-on" learner who prefers to touch, move, build, or draw what you learn, and you tend to learn better when some type of physical activity is involved.
- Kinesthetic learners will show a preference for demonstrations and physical activity involving bodily movement.

100 Willingness To Communicate (WTC)***

an underlying continuum representing the predisposition toward or away from communicating, given the choice

101 Working memory***

a construct that refers to a temporary memory storage system used to process and rehearse linguistic input and language information retrieved from long-term memory
It is conceptually similar to short-term memory; however, working memory is limited in its capacity, both in terms of the amount of information it can hold (around seven items for most individuals) and the amount of processing it can do. Some studies have found that larger working memories aid learning by enabling learners to *notice* more corrective feedback or to *notice* relationships between related elements in a sentence that are separated by intervening words or morphemes. (**Ex** subject-verb agreement)

※ **Read the following descriptions and fill in the blanks.**

01 _____ _____

a style in which an individual is relatively well suited to withstand or manage a high degree of uncertainty in a linguistic context

02 _____

the subjective feeling of tension, apprehension, and nervousness connected to an arousal of the autonomic nervous system, and associated with feelings of uneasiness, frustration, self-doubt, apprehension or worries. (facilitative _____, and debilitative _____)

03 _____

Learners may choose not to use certain L2 structures(topic, voca, grammar) if those structures are difficult or problematic to them. Instead they may use language that is simpler and easier for them to produce. THIS may therefore result in language that is more accurate or fluent, but the language may be less complex or advanced.
(a) (of a topic) in a conversation, steering others away from an unwanted topic
(b) (of a language form) a strategy that leads to refraining from producing a form that speaker may not know, often through an alternative form

04 _____ _____ (communication strategies)

① avoidance: avoiding a topic, concept, grammatical construction, or phonological element that poses difficulty
② circumlocution: describing an object or idea with a definition
③ approximation: using an alternative term which expresses the meaning of the target lexical item as closely as possible
④ word coinage: creating a nonexistent L2 word based on a supposed rule
⑤ prefabricated patterns: using memorized stock phrases, usually for "survival" purposes
⑥ code-switching: using an L1 word with L1 pronunciation while speaking in L2
⑦ appeal to authority: asking for aid either directly or indirectly (usually direct appeal)
⑧ literal translation: translating a lexical item, an idiom, or a structure from the learners' L1 to L2
⑨ keeping the floor: using fillers or hesitation devices to fill pauses and to gain time to think (well, now let's see, uh, as a matter of fact)
⑩ foreignizing: using an L1 word by adjusting it to L2 phonology and/or morphologically (adding it to a L2 suffix)
⑪ nonlinguistic signals: mime, gesture, facial expression, or sound imitation

05 _____ _____

errors that are <u>grammatically</u> well formed at the sentence level but <u>not interpretable within the context</u> of communication; discourse errors. THEY only become apparent when a larger stretch of discourse is considered, rather than only inspecting the sentence.

> **Ex**
> We're here for three weeks.
> meaning: We're staying here for three weeks in total.
> 화자의 의도: We've been here for three weeks.

06 _____

"putting yourself into someone else's shoes," reaching beyond the self to understand what another person is thinking or feeling

07 _____

the extent to which a person has a deep-seated need to receive ego enhancement, self-esteem, and a sense of wholeness from other people, as opposed to receiving that affirmation within oneself

08 _____ _____

the tendency to be "dependent" on the total field so that the parts embedded in the filed are not easily perceived, although that total field is perceived more clearly as a unified whole (=field sensitivity)(**Ex** global learners)

09 _____

an individual's tendency to be comfortable making quick or gambling decisions Taking linguistic risks in the face of possible error. Taking initiative in conversations. (see also **reflectivity**)

10 _____

apprehension over one's self-identity or fear of showing self-doubt, leading to building mechanisms of protective self-defense

11 _____

learner language that emphasizes the separateness of a second language learner's system, a system that has a structurally intermediate status between the native and target languages

12 _____   _____

This type of motivation is internal to the learner. It is characterized by positive feelings towards the language, its speakers and their culture. (Ex) studying Japanese because a person likes anime and manga; learning a language because a person enjoys the challenge of analysing a language) For a time it was thought THIS was superior to extrinsic motivation; however there is no conclusive evidence that this is always the case. Also, the distinction between the two types of motivation is not always clear. THIS is similar to integrative motivation, a term introduced by Gardner and Lambert. (1972)

13 _____

the extent to which a person derives a sense of wholeness and fulfillment from within, apart from a reflection of this self from other people

14 _____   _____

the identity a person develops in reference to the language he or she speaks

15 _____ _____

errors that <u>do not prevent a message from being understood</u>, usually due to a minor violation of one segment of a sentence, allowing the hearer/reader to make an accurate guess about the intended meaning

16 _____ _____

strategic options that relate to <u>one's "executive" functions</u>; strategies that involve planning for learning, thinking about the learning process as it is taking place, monitoring of one's production or comprehension, and evaluating learning after an activity is completed. - *planning, organizing, monitoring, evaluating*

17 _____ _____

errors that are <u>unquestionaly ungrammatical at the sentence level</u>
THEY can be detected by inspecting the sentence or utterance in which it occurs.

18 _____

willingness to <u>gamble</u>, to try out hunches about a language <u>with the possibility of being wrong</u>

19 _____

<u>belief in one's own capabilities</u> to perform a specific activity

20 _____

self-appraisal, self-confidence, knowledge of oneself, usually categorized into "global" (overall), "situational/specific" (in a general context), and "task" (particular activities within a context)

21 _____   _____

strategies that help learners regulate and control emotions, motivations, and attitudes towards learning, as well as help learners learn through contact and interaction with others (strategic options relating to social-mediating activity and interacting with others)

22 _____   _____   (≒ **sociocultural competence**)

ability to use or apply sociocultural rules of discourse in a language

23 _____

a concept that refers to the fact that a learner's interlanguage system may cease develop before it achieves target-like accuracy
However, unlike *fossilization*, THIS does not imply that a learner's knowledge of a specific structure cannot develop further, but rather it implies that there is no further learning at the moment. It is typically used to refer to specific linguistic structures, rather than to the learners interlanguage system as a whole. THIS acknowledges that as long as a learner is alive, there may be the possibilities for further L2 development. (see also *postsystematic stage*, and *fossilization*)

24 - _____ learners tend to prefer reading and studying charts, drawings, and other graphic information.
- _____ learners prefer listening to lectures and audiotapes.
- _____ learner is a "hands-on" learner who prefers to touch, move, build, or draw what you learn, and you tend to learn better when some type of physical activity is involved.
- _____ learners will show a preference for demonstrations and physical activity involving bodily movement.

02

25 _____   _____   _____

an underlying continuum representing the predisposition toward or away from communicating, given the choice

Answers

01 Ambiguity tolerance	**14** Language ego
02 Anxiety	**15** Local errors
03 Avoidance	**16** Metacognitive strategy
04 Compensatory strategies	**17** Overt errors
05 Covert errors	**18** Risk taking
06 Empathy	**19** Self-efficacy
07 Extroversion	**20** Self-esteem
08 Field dependence	**21** Socioaffective strategies
09 Impulsivity	**22** Sociolinguistic competence
10 Inhibition	**23** Stabilization
11 Interlanguage	**24** Visual, Auditory, Tactile, Kinesthetic
12 Intrinsic motivation	**25** Willingness to communicate
13 Introversion	

Note

Teaching-related Terms

(Teaching Culture, Materials & Methods, Communicative Competence)

※ **Review the following Key Terms list and put a checkmark next to Terms that you do not know the exact meaning.**

- ☐ Acculturation
- ☐ Acculturation model
- ☐ Action research
- ☐ Adjunct model
- ☐ Anomie
- ☐ Artifact
- ☐ Audio-motor unit
- ☐ Audiolingual Method (ALM)
- ☐ Autonomy
- ☐ Blended learning
- ☐ Classroom management
- ☐ Communicative
- ☐ Communicative competence (Canale and Swain, 1983)
- ☐ Communicative competence (Littlewood, 2011)
- ☐ Communicative task (Prahbu, 1987)
  ① information-gap activity ② opinion-gap activity ③ reasoning-gap activity
- ☐ Communities of Practice (CoP)
- ☐ Community Language Learning (CLL)
- ☐ Computer-adaptive Testing (CAT)
- ☐ Computer-assisted Language Learning (CALL)
- ☐ Computer-mediated Communication (CMC)
- ☐ Content-based Instruction (CBI)
- ☐ Cooperative learning
- ☐ Corpus linguistics
- ☐ Culture assimilator

- ☐ Culture capsule
- ☐ Culture island
- ☐ Culture shock
- ☐ Digital literacy
- ☐ Discovery learning
- ☐ Elaboration
- ☐ English only (debate)
- ☐ Experiential learning
- ☐ Eye contact
- ☐ Flipped learning
- ☐ Immersion
- ☐ Inner circle
- ☐ Input modification
- ☐ Kinesics
- ☐ Kinesthetics
- ☐ Language competence (Bachman, 1990)
- ☐ Learner-centered instruction
- ☐ Lexical approach
- ☐ Lexico-grammatical approach
- ☐ Macroskills
- ☐ Metalanguage
- ☐ Microskills
- ☐ Mobile-assisted Language Learning (MALL)
- ☐ Modified input
- ☐ Multimodal communication
- ☐ Natural Approach
- ☐ Needs analysis / Needs assessment
- ☐ Notional-functional syllabus

03

- [ ] Objective
- [ ] Objective needs
- [ ] Oculesics
- [ ] Olfactory
- [ ] Online planning
- [ ] Optimal distance model
- [ ] Outer circle
- [ ] Pacing
- [ ] Pair work
- [ ] Perceived social distance
- [ ] PPP
- [ ] Procedure
- [ ] Process-oriented syllabus
- [ ] Product-oriented syllabus
- [ ] Project-based learning
- [ ] Psychological distance
- [ ] Realia
- [ ] Sheltered model
- [ ] Simplification
- [ ] Situation analysis
- [ ] Social distance
- [ ] Sociocultural awareness
- [ ] Sociopragmatics
- [ ] Speech acts
- [ ] Spiral learning
- [ ] Strategies-based Instruction (SBI)
- [ ] Structural Syllabus
- [ ] Subject-integrated class

- ☐ Subjective needs
- ☐ Sustained Deep Learning (SDL)
- ☐ Syllabus
- ☐ Task-based Language Teaching (TBLT)
- ☐ Teachability hypothesis
- ☐ Teacher's roles ① Controller ② Director ③ Manager ④ Facilitator ⑤ Resource
- ☐ Technique(s)
- ☐ Textbook adaptation
  ① adding ② deleting ③ modifying ④ simplifying ⑤ reordering
- ☐ Theme-based instruction
- ☐ Think-aloud strategy / technique
- ☐ Total Physical Response (TPR)
- ☐ Translanguaging
- ☐ Uncertainty avoidance
- ☐ World Englishes

01   Acculturation***

cultural adaptation
John Schumann's acculturation model states that some L2 learners do not progress beyond the early stages of linguistic acquisition with a target language because of social and psychological distance between the speaker's culture and the target culture. A lack of acculturation or cultural adaptation, according to the model, can lead to linguistic fossilization or pidginization. (Ellis)

02   Acculturation model***

a theory of L2 acquisition developed by Schumann that the rate and level of ultimate success of second language acquisition in naturalistic settings (without instruction) is a function of the degree to which learners acculturate to the target language community
According to this model, L2 acquisition is one aspect of acculturation. It contends that learners will succeed in second language acquisition only to the extent that they acculturate into the group that speaks the target language natively. The closer they feel to the target speech community, the better learners will become 'acculturated' and the more successful their language learning will be. In this model, instruction is set apart from acculturation and is less important in the SLA process than acculturation. This model lost favor by the early 1980s as research increasingly turned its attention toward linguistic and psycholinguistic approaches to explaining acquisition phenomena.

03   Action research***

(sometimes, teacher research, or classroom research) the systematic investigation of an issue, problem, or pedagogical question in a "live" classroom setting with students, and reporting on the findings of the investigation
It is conducted by L2 teachers in their own classrooms in order to address questions that are particularly relevant to their own teaching contexts. It is often viewed as an iterative process in which teachers identify a topic of investigation related to their teaching, evaluate this topic, and then modify their teaching in light of their findings. (Four steps: *planning, acting, observing, and reflecting*)

04 Activity [B]

a reasonably unified set of student behaviors, limited in time, preceded by some direction from the teacher, with a particular objective

05 Adjunct model (of content-based language teaching)***

linking subject-matter teachers and language teachers in content-based courses affect emotion or feeling

06 Anomie***

feelings of social uncertainty, dissatisfaction, or "homelessness" as individuals lose some of the bonds of a native culture but are not yet fully acculturated in the new culture

07 Approach [E]

theoretical position about the nature of language and of language learning and teaching

08 Artifact(s)***

(특히, 비언어적 의사소통의 상황에서) external factors of a person, such as clothing and ornamentation, and their effect on communication

09 Artifact study***

It is designed to help students discern the cultural significance of certain unfamiliar objects from the target culture. The activity involves students in giving descriptions and forming hypotheses about the function of the unknown object.

10 Audiolingual Method (ALM)***

a language teaching method that emphasized <u>oral production, pattern drills</u>, and conditioning through <u>repetition</u>

11 Audio-motor unit***

a language teaching method relying on physical or kinesthetic movement accompanied by language practice. commend-based instruction, imperative commands given to learners, learners respond with actions.

(a) It includes a particular sequence of commands, all centering on a single topic.

Topic : Set the table

"Go to the cupboard, open the cupboard door, find the largest bowl, take it out, set it on the table."

(b) The teacher demonstrates the appropriate responses to the commands, <u>using whatever realia are available</u> to make the actions comprehensible.

(c) The students are invited to comply with the commands.

Preparation: fork, napkin, meat, knife, plate, table, glass, wine, bread

You are in a restaurant. / Pick up your napkin. / Unfold it. / Put it in your lap. / Pick up your fork with your left hand.

12 Autonomy***

<u>individual effort and action</u> through which learners <u>initiate language, problem solving, strategic action, and the generation of linguistic input</u>

13 Blended learning***

Blended learning involves online and face-to-face instruction. Both are used alongside each other in order to provide a comprehensive learning experience. For example, a trainer might give learners a list of online resources they can use to broaden their understanding of the topic, or ask them to complete an online group project that centers on a subject they are currently discussing. In the case of blended learning, online materials do not take the place of face-to-face instruction; instead, the two modalities complement one another. They truly "blend" in order to create an enriched online training environment for the learner.

14 Classroom-based assessment Ⓔ

instruments either created or adapted to assess classroom/course objectives

15 Classroom language Ⓑ

academic discourse typical of linguistic exchanges in classrooms between teacher and students and among students (Ex in small group work), often involving *directions, questions, discussions, agreeing and disagreeing*

16 Classroom management Ⓑ

the process of ensuring that classroom lessons run smoothly considering a wide range of factors from the physical arrangement of a classroom, to teaching styles and philosophy, to classroom energy

17 Communicative Ⓑ

Student responses are meaningful, real-world related, open-ended, and unpredictable.

18 Communicative competence (Canale and Swain, 1983) Ⓑ

a term used to refer to a learner's ability to use language
The term, popularized in SLA, refers to learners' language knowledge that includes more than just grammatical accuracy or an idealized competence in the language. Communicative competence is seen as being composed of several difference components: linguistic competence, sociolinguistic competence, discourse competence, strategic competence.

① **Grammatical competence:** Knowledge of lexical items and of rules of morphology, syntax, sentence-grammar semantics, and phonology. It is the competence we associate with mastering the linguistic code of a language, the **linguistic competence** referred to by Hymes (1972) and Paulston (1974)

② **Sociolinguistic competence:** The ability to follow sociocultural rules of language. This requires an understanding of the social context in which language is used: the roles of the participants, the information they share, and the function of the interaction.

③ **Discourse competence:** The ability to connect sentences in stretches of discourse and to form a meaningful whole out of a series of utterances. With its inter-sentential relationships, discourse encompasses everything from simple spoken conversations to lengthy written texts (articles, books, etc)

④ **Strategic competence:** The ability to use verbal and nonverbal communicative techniques to compensate for breakdowns in communication or insufficient competence. It includes the ability to make "repairs" and to sustain communication through paraphrase, circumlocution, repetition, avoidance, and guessing.

19 Communicative competence (Littlewood, 2011) Ⓑ

① **Linguistic competence** (=grammatical competence)
② **Discourse competence** (=textual competence)
③ **Pragmatic competence** (=strategic competence): the ability to use linguistic resources to convey and interpret meanings in real situations, including those where learners encounter problems due to gaps in their knowledge
④ **Sociolinguistic competence** (same as Canale and Swain's definition)
⑤ **Sociocultural competence:** cultural knowledge and assumptions that affect the exchange of meanings

20　Communicative task (Prahbu, 1987)^{***}

① **Information-gap activities** are those that involve the transfer of information from one person to another, from one form to another or from one place to another. For example, two students might have different schedules, but they want to find time to get together to have tea. They need to get relevant information from each other to determine when they are both free, as well as when the available times coincide with when a tea house is open. This type of activity allows students to request information, ask for clarification and negotiate both meaning, particularly when misunderstandings occur, and appropriate conclusions to the task.

② **Opinion-gap activities** are those that ask students to convey their own personal preferences, feelings or ideas about a particular situation. On a higher level, you might ask them to take part in a discussion or debate about a political or social issue. On a lower level, you might ask them to complete a story. In these types of activities, there is no right or wrong answer, and, therefore, there is no objective means by which to judge outcomes, outside of whether what the students do or say addresses the task at hand. You might require them to speak or write for a certain amount (words or time) and you might ask them to use certain constructions. Otherwise, assessment is subjective rather than objective.

③ **Reasoning-gap activities** are those in which you ask your students to derive some information from that which you give them. They are required to comprehend and convey information, much as in an information gap activity, but the information that they are asked to convey is not exactly the same that they comprehend. They are asked to use reason and logic to decide what information to convey and what resolution to make for the problem at hand. For example, you might ask your students to make a decision between speed and cost or cost and quality, given a certain situation and various constraints.

21　Communities of Practice (CoP) ®

group of people who share a common interest in a particular domain
Teachers of varying degrees of experience carry out their roles as practicing professionals who learn from each other. Professional development can be fulfilled not through a transmission model of education, but through a process model where teachers learn and continue to develop their skills, in dialogue with a professional community.

22 Community Language Learning (CLL)***

language teaching method that emphasizes interpersonal relationships, inductive learning, and views the teacher as a "counselor"

23 Computer-adaptive Testing (CAT) (=tailored testing)***

Computerized adaptive testing (CAT) is a form of computer-based test that adapts to the examinee's ability level. For this reason, it has also been called tailored testing. In other words, it is a form of computer-administered test in which the next item or set of items selected to be administered depends on the correctness of the test taker's responses to the most recent items administered.

24 Computer-assisted Language Learning (CALL)***

the subfield of applied linguistics concerned with the use of computers for teaching and learning a second language

25 Computer-mediated Communication (CMC)***

communication through the use of two or more electronic devices such as computers, tablet PCs, and smart phones
Commonly used formats are e-mail, video, audio, or text chatting supported by social software. (Ex applications)

26 Concordance***

(검색해 놓은 결과물) It is an alphabetical list of the principal words used in a book or body of work, listing every instance of each word with its immediate context. The sample of concordance can provide students with instances of real language use helping learners to know how to use language that is appropriate in different contexts.

27 Concordancing***

searching for words in context and collocations
Indexing of words that enables one to reference words in the multiple possible contexts in which they appear in spoken or written language.

28 Content-based Instruction (CBI) / Content-based Language Teaching (CBLT)***

an umbrella term for a multifaceted approach to second or foreign language teaching that ... shares a common point of departure - the integration of language teaching aims with content instruction. The concurrent study of language and subject matter, with the form and sequence of language presentation dictated by content material.

① Immersion model: a type of education that involves placing L2 learners in an environment primarily comprised of the target language. Learners study academic content, such as math, science, and history in the target language. (English L2 speaking children attended school classes conducted in French.)

② Sheltered model (sheltered-language instruction): involves the deliberate separation of L2 students from native speakers of the target language for the purpose of content instruction. For L2 students whose language proficiency is not quite able to handle subject-matter content in the L1 of the educational system, they provide opportunities for them to master content standards with added language assistance. In such cases, the teacher of a school subject (science, history) modifies the presentation of material to help L2 learners process the content. Pre-teaching difficult vocabulary, suggesting reading comprehension strategies, explaining certain grammatical structures, and offering form-focused feedback are among techniques that have shown to be helpful.

③ Adjunct model: linking subject-matter teachers and language teachers in content-based courses (A team-teaching model), you are first and foremost teaching science or math, and secondarily teaching language.

④ Theme-based instruction(주제중심학습): When language courses are organized around meaningful situations or topic, they may be said to be theme-based, sometimes referred to as topic-based curricula. Theme-based instruction can serve multiple interests of students in a classroom and can offer a focus on content while still adhering to institutional requirements for coverage of grammatical criteria. Brinton put theme-based teaching under the rubric of content-based language teaching (but there are variations) L2 textbook, at the intermediate to advanced levels, offer theme-based courses of study. Challenging topics in these textbooks engage the curiosity and increase motivation of students as they grapple with an array of real-life issues ranging from simple to complex and also improve their linguistic skills across all four domains of listening, speaking, reading and writing.

> **Cf**
>
> *** Subject-integrated class**
> 교과 간 통합수업 내용중심 교육의 약화된 모델로 내용과 언어 모두를 가르치는 데 초점을 두고 있다. 주제중심의 교육은 학생들의 흥미를 고려하여 주제를 선정하고 이와 관련된 활동을 바탕으로 영어를 지도하는 방법이다. 따라서 다양한 주제를 중심으로 이와 관련된 타 교과 과목과 통합하여 영어를 지도할 수 있다. Brown (2001)은 전통적인 언어 수업에 대한 대안으로 주제나 소재를 중심으로 수업을 수행할 경우 자동화, 유의적인 학습, 내적 동기 및 의사소통 능력과 관련된 원리에 입각하여 실용적이고 효과적으로 언어를 가르칠 수 있다고 언급하고 있다. 즉 다른 교과의 소재를 활용하여 영어 수업을 진행하기 때문에 그 교과의 내용을 예습 혹은 복습하는 효과를 얻을 수 있을 뿐만 아니라 영어로 다양한 분야의 내용을 배울 수 있다는 효과가 있다. 따라서 이 교육방법에서는 수업시간에 다루게 될 주제나 소재의 선별이 매우 중요하다.

29   Cooperative learning***

model of education in which students work together in pairs and groups, share information, and come to each other's aid, as opposed to *teacher-centered instruction* (see also **learner-centered instruction**)

30   Corpus linguistics***

an approach to linguistic research that relies on computer analyses of a collection of text, written, transcribed speech or both stored in electronic form and analyzed with digital software

31 Corpus-based teaching***

using corpora to inform curriculum and lesson designs (see also **corpus linguistics**)

32 Culture assimilator***

culture training programs first developed at the University of Illinois in the 1960s
The format of assimilators is as follows. An episode is described followed by 4 or 5 explanations of why there is a problem or difficulty. For example, why do people from culture A behave that way? The trainee selects the explanation that s/he thinks is best. The explanations are selected such that when people from culture B are learning about culture A most of the explanations are frequently given by people in culture B and one explanation comes from culture A. After the trainee selects an explanation s/he is asked to turn to a page that gives feedback about each explanation. If the explanation selected by the trainee is incorrect, the trainee is told that this is not the best explanation, and to try another explanation. When the trainee picks the correct explanation, the feedback is extensive, describing cultural similarities and differences between cultures A and B. Assimilators that use feedback that includes culture theory, such as the differences between collectivist and individualist cultures, are especially effective. Gradually, the trainee from culture B starts thinking like the people from culture A. In a way, s/he learns to get "into the shoes" of the people from the other culture.

33 Culture capsule***

It is a brief description, usually one or two paragraphs, of some aspect of the target culture, followed by or incorporated with contrasting information about the students' native culture. Culture capsules can be written by teachers or students.

34 Culture island***

A culture island is an area in the classroom where posters, maps, objects, and pictures or people, lifestyles, or customs of other cultures are displayed to attract learners' attention, evoke comments, and help students develop a mental image.

35 Culture shock***

in the process of acculturation, phenomena involving mild irritability, depression, anger, or possibly deep <u>psychological crisis</u> due to the foreignness of the new cultural milieu Culture shock is an experience a person may have when one moves to a cultural environment which is different from one's own; it is also <u>the personal disorientation</u> a person may feel when <u>experiencing an unfamiliar way of life</u> due to immigration or a visit to a new country, a move between social environments, or simply transition to another type of life. One of the most common causes of culture shock involves individuals in a foreign environment. Culture shock can be described as consisting of at least one of four distinct phases: honeymoon, negotiation, adjustment, and adaptation.

36 Culture stress***

Culture stress is the <u>ongoing pressure</u> that you live with when you live in another culture or country than the one in which you were raised. (**Cf**) anomie: a feeling of being torn between two cultures, and not feeling properly part of either)

37 Curriculum ⓔ

a course of study that includes specifications of topics, forms, assignments, and schedules for completion; also, a group of separate courses within a program (see **syllabus**)

38 Digital literacy***

It is the ability to understand and use information in multiple formats from a wide variety of sources when it is presented via computers. (Gilster)

39 Direct method***

a language teaching method popular in the early twentieth century that emphasized direct target language use, oral communication skills, and inductive grammar, without recourse to translation from the first language

40 Directive (approaches to teaching) ©

The teacher is more in control of lessons than students.

41 Discovery learning***

the concept that when learners are spurred to induce language. or other content, as opposed to being told by the teacher, greater retention results.

42 Elaboration***

see **modified input**

43 English only (debate)***

a term for a movement and philosophy in the US that seeks to make English the official language of the US and to discourage the use of bilingual education

44 Experiential learning***

instruction that highlights giving students concrete experiences in which they must use language in order to fulfill the objectives of a lesson

It is an engaged learning process whereby students "learn by doing" and by reflecting on the experience. This type of learning highlights giving learners concrete experiences in which they must use language in order to fulfill the objectives of a lesson. (Contextualize language, integrate skills, authentic purposes)

hands on projects, field trips, research projects, creating a video

45 Extra-class work ®

assignments that a student is given to do outside the regular class hours, commonly called "homework"

46 Eye contact***

nonverbal feature involving what one looks at and how one looks at another person in face-to-face communication

47 Flipped learning***

The flipped classroom is a pedagogical model in which the typical lecture and homework elements of a course are reversed. Flipped learning, which is also known as a flipped classroom, is a bit more clear-cut. There is a divide between the technology and face-to-face elements of the learning experience. A learner is asked to watch an e-Learning video or participate in another online learning exercise BEFORE coming to class. In the classroom the new materials are explored at-length. In most cases, the knowledge that is learned online is applied in the classroom.

48 Functional syllabus[***]

see **Notional-Functional syllabus**

49 Goal [B]

the overall purpose toward which a course or a lesson is directed and is intended to achieve

50 Grammar translation method [E]

a language teaching method in which the central focus is on grammatical rules, paradigms, and vocabulary memorization as the basis for translating from one language to another

51 Group dynamics[***]

the way that two or more students behave with each other in a particular classroom environment, which also influences how they relate to each other and how effectively communicate and work together

52 Group work [B]

a variety of techniques in which two or more students are assigned a task that involves collaboration and self-initiated language

53 Immersion***

educational model that typically provides the majority of subject-matter content through the medium of the L2 (see also **CBI**)

54 Inner circle***

countries traditionally considered to be dominated by native speakers of English
Ex United States, United Kingdom, Australia, New Zealand

55 Input modification***

Tony Lynch proposes some most common input modifications of teacher talk which are suitable especially for elementary or pre-intermediate level:
① lexical modification: use of more common vocabulary / avoidance of idioms / use of nouns rather than pronouns
② syntactic modification: shorter utterances / less complex utterances / more regular surface structure / increased use of present tense

56 Kinesics***

body language, gesture, eye contact, and other physical features of nonverbal communication Every culture and language uses gesture or kinesics, in unique but clearly interpretable ways
Sometimes a gesture that is appropriate in one culture is obscene or insulting in another.

57 Kinesthetics***

In nonverbal communication, conventions for how to touch others and where to touch them touching, sometimes referred to as kinesthetics, also called **haptics**, is culturally loaded aspect of non-verbal communication. How we touch and where we touch them is sometimes the most misunderstood aspect of nonverbal communication.

58 Language competence (Bachman, 1990)***

① **Organizational competence**: the rules and systems that govern what we can do with the forms of language, whether they be sentence-level (grammatical) rules or rules that specify how we string sentences together (discourse)
    (a) grammatical competence
    (b) discourse competence (textual competence)
② **Pragmatic competence**: includes functional aspects of language (illocutionary competence) and sociolinguistic aspects which deal with such considerations as politeness, formality, metaphor, register, and culturally related aspects of language
    (a) illocutionary competence
    (b) socioliguistic competence

59 Learner-centered instruction***

model of education with a focus on learners' needs and goals and individual differences in a supportive atmosphere that offers students choices and some control

60 Lexical approach***

a language teaching method that emphasized the importance of words/vocabulary in SLA The lexical approach is a way of analysing and teaching language based on the idea that a language is made up of lexical units rather than grammatical structures. The units are words, chunks formed by collocations, and fixed phrases.
(a) The phrase 'Rescue attempts are being hampered by bad weather' is a chunk of language, and almost a fixed phrase. It is formed by the collocations 'Rescue' + 'attempt', 'rescue attempt' + 'hampered', 'hampered' + 'by', 'hampered by' + 'bad weather'.
(b) In the classroom A simple activity to incorporate the lexical approach is to encourage learners to identify and record lexical chunks and fixed phrases in texts they read.

61 Lexico-grammatical approach***

A view that lexis and grammar are two inherently connected parts of a single entity and should not be treated separately. "Vocabulary and grammatical structures are interdependent; so much so that it is possible to say with some justification that words have their own grammar." This interdependency of lexis and grammar is evident everywhere in language. For example, lexical verbs have valency (v+sth) patterns: some verbs can be used with a direct object, or with both a direct object and an indirect object, others need no object at all.

62 Macroskills ®

skills that are technically at the discourse level

63 Metalanguage***

the language that is used to talk about language
It may consist of both technical or non-technical terms. Examples of technical metalinguistic terms in SLA would be present perfect tense and subject verb agreement. Examples of non-technical metalinguistic terms would include word and sentence.

64 Microskills ®

skills that are at the sentence level

65 Mobile-assisted Language Learning (MALL)***

the use of mobile technologies (**Ex** smart phones, tablets) for language learning, especially in situations where device portability offers particular advantages (see also **CALL**)

66　Modified input***

input that has been changed in some way from its original, authentic form
① simplification: The language is made less complex by using shorter sentences, simpler grammatical forms or more commonly occurring vocabulary. There has been some suggestion that simplified talk may help with learner comprehension but that it is not helpful for longer-term development.
② elaboration: It includes restating ideas in different ways or repeating segments of the input. Elaborated talk has been shown to have a positive effect on acquisition.

67　Multimodal communication***

sending and receiving messages through several modes, such as text, visuals, audio, and touch, that are available when creating *ePortfolios, websites, visual presentation slides, research posters, and other materials*
Students can be encouraged to create their own websites, blogs, and online communities using *multimodal communication*, which can be turned into active **project-based learning**.

68　Native English-speaking Teachers (NESTs) ©

teachers whose L1 is English

69　Native informant***

Native informants can be valuable resources to the classroom teacher, both as sources of current information about the target culture and as linguistic models for students. Students can develop a set of questions they would like to ask before native speakers come to the class.

70   Natural approach***

: a language teaching method that simulates child language acquisition by emphasizing communication, comprehensible input, kinesthetic activities, and virtually no grammatical analysis (also natural method)

: a term for a number of language-teaching methods which were developed in the nineteenth century as a reaction to the grammar translation method

These methods emphasized:

(a) the use of the spoken language

(b) the use of objects and actions in teaching the meanings of words and structures

(c) the need to make language teaching follow the natural principles of first language learning

The natural approach aims to develop communicative skills, and it is primarily intended to be used with beginning learners. It is presented as a set of principles that can apply to a wide range of learners and teaching situations, and concrete objectives depend on the specific context in which it is used. Terrell outlines three basic principles of the approach:

"Focus of instruction is on communication rather than its form."

"*Speech* production comes slowly and is never forced."

"*Early speech* goes through natural stages. (yes or no response, one-word answers, lists of words, short phrases, complete sentences)"

71   Needs analysis / Needs assessment***

Needs analysis is the process of specifying the learners' language needs in advance of designing a course of them. The analysis can then be used to materials, and also the methodology. Finally, the needs analysis can be used in the design of assessment and evaluation procedures.

Needs assessment refers to a systematic process for determining and addressing needs, overall purposes of the course, or "gaps" that the course is intended to fill, and the opinions of both course designers and students about their reasons for developing/taking the course.

It is important to identify at least two types of needs: **objective** and **subjective**

72 Nondirective (approaches to teaching) [Ⓔ]

using more inductive, student-centered approaches

73 Nonnative English-speaking Teachers (NNESTs) [Ⓔ]

teachers whose L1 is not English

74 Notional-functional syllabus (=functional syllabus)***

a language course that attends primarily to functions as organizing elements of a foreign language curriculum
* **Notion:** general (existence, space, time, quality, quantity) / specific (situations, personal identification, name, address, phone number,..)
* **Function:** identifying, reporting, denying, accepting, declining, asking permission, apologizing

75 Objective [Ⓑ]

explicit statement of what students will gain from a lesson and their expected performance, which will demonstrate achievement of learning outcomes

76 Objective needs***

Objective needs are those that can be relatively easily measured, qualified, or specified with agreement by administrators on what constitutes defined needs. These are analyzed through test data (including learner language samples), questionnaire results, teacher reports, observations, and interviews of teachers and students.
* demographic data on learners, including language ability, interests, etc
* needs expressed in terms of proficiency levels
* language skills to be addressed
* what learners need to do in English (target contexts for English use)

77 Oculesics***

nonverbal communication involving eye contact and eye "gestures" to signal meaning

78 Olfactory***

pertaining to one's sense of smell; in nonverbal communication the effect of natural and artificial odors on communication

79 Online planning (on-line planning, within-task planning) ©

the type of planning that learners engage in while they are conducting a task
As such there is only limited time for them to plan their language production. Consequently, learners have to rely primarily on their proceduralized or implicit L2 knowledge, and they are able to access only the most basic grammatical rules to help them with language production. Online planning contrasts with pre-task planning, and is a variable that is investigated in task-based language teaching. (Task difficulty에 영향을 주는 변수)

80 Optimal distance model***

the hypothesis that an adult who fails to master a second language in a second culture may have failed to *synchronize linguistic and cultural development*
A delay, well into a stage of adaptation or integration, in achieving communicative success in the L2 may result in lower motivation to succeed and possibly *fossilization of language*. (a culturally based critical period is independent of the age of the learner)

81 Outer circle***

countries that use English as a common lingua franca and in which English is for many people nativized **Ex** India, Singapore, the Philippines, Nigeria, Ghana

82   Pacing [Ⓔ]

the comfort level of a lesson in terms of rhythm and speed
As you are drafting step-by-step procedures, you need to look at how the lesson holds
together as a whole.

·Is the lesson as a whole paced adequately?

  -Activities are neither too long nor too short.

  -Various techniques should flow together.

    (**Ex**) smooth flow: 5minutes each of whole-class work, pair work, whole class work,
      group work, pair work, whole-class work, etc.)

  -Well transition from one activity to the next.

·Four considerations in drafting lesson plans: variety, sequencing, pacing, and timing

03

83   Pair work***

group work in groups of two, but usually involves less complex and briefer tasks

84   Pedagogical task(s) (=pedagogic task(s))***

any of a sequence of techniques designed ultimately to teach students to perform the
target task

85   Perceived social distance***

the cognitive and affective proximity that one perceives, as opposed to an objectively
measured or "actual" distance between cultures (see **social distance**)
Instead of trying to measure actual social distance, Bill Acton (1979) devised a measure
of perceived social distance. In the case of some learners there was an optimal perceived
social distance ratio (neither too close nor too far from the target culture) that typified
the successful language learners.

86   PPP: Presentation → Practice → Production[***]

a method of language instruction that involves the <u>explicit presentation</u> of specific linguistic forms, <u>such as vocabulary items or grammar rules</u>
This presentation is followed by <u>controlled learner practice</u> of the target forms. Finally, <u>freer production</u> in using the forms is allowed. PPP is often associated with more traditional types of L2 instruction, in which the target language is presented in a largely decontextualized, non-communicative context. it does not allow learners to use the language items for primarily communicative purposes.

87   Procedure [E]

a series of actions that are performed either by a teacher or students in a certain order <u>during the lesson</u>

88   Process [B]

a progression of procedures (steps, stages, strategies, milestones) in learners' <u>language development</u> (versus the end product)

89   Process-oriented syllabus[***]

the syllabus focusing on the skills and processes involved in learning language
(Ex task-based syllabus, learner-centered syllabus, content syllabus)

90   Product [B]

<u>the ultimate or end result</u> of a set of learning efforts; for example, a final "paper" or the summation of abilities at the end of a course of study (versus the process of progressive achievement of that end)

91 Product-oriented syllabus***

the syllabus focusing on things learned at the end of the learning process/outcomes
(Ex structural syllabus, situational syllabus, notional-functional syllabus)

92 Program ©

a collection of classes or courses offered within a single institution that lead to a
certificate or degree

93 Project-based Learning (PBL)***

Project-based Learning (PBL) involves students designing, developing, and constructing
hands-on solutions to a problem. The educational value of PBL is that it aims to
build students' creative capacity to work through difficult or ill-structured problems,
commonly in small teams. Typically, PBL takes students through the following phases
or steps:
(a) Identifying a problem
(b) Agreeing on or devising a solution and potential solution path to the problem (i.e.,
how to achieve the solution)
(c) Designing and developing a prototype of the solution
(d) Refining the solution based on feedback from experts, instructors, and/or peers
Depending on the goals of the instructor, the size and scope of the project can vary
greatly. Students may complete the four phases listed above over the course of many
weeks, or even several times within a single class period.

94 Psychological distance***

(in acculturation model) one of the factors determine acculturation
It concerns the extent to which individual learners are comfortable with the learning task and constitutes, therefore, a personal rather than a group dimension. Among the factors which affect psychological distance are language shock, culture shock, motivation, and ego permeability. The social factors are primary. The psychological factors mainly come into play where social distance is indeterminate. (i.e., where social factors constitute neither a clearly positive nor a negative influence on acculturation)

95 Realia***

Realia in EFL terms refers to any real objects we use in the classroom to bring the class to life. (usually for teaching vocabulary)

96 Series method ⓔ

language teaching method created by Gouin, in which learners practiced a number of connected "series" of sentences, which together formed a meaningful story or sequence of events

97 Sheltered model (sheltered-language instruction)***

the deliberate separation of L2 students from native speakers of the target language for the purpose of content instruction (see also **CBI**)

98 Simplification***

see **modified input**

99   Situation analysis [E]

a study of information about the target educational setting, characteristics of class, faculty, and students, governance of course content and materials, and assessment methods (also called as environment analysis)

The first - or perhaps among the first - steps in course design is an analysis of the setting, the audience, and needs of the students.

A second step in the process of developing or understanding a course centers on the needs that the course presumes to address, which is **needs analysis**.

100   Social distance***

the perception that learners have of themselves in relation to speakers of the target language

If learners feel an affinity for the target language speakers and culture, then the social distance is lessened. In contrast, if learners feel isolated from the target language culture, or antagonistic to it, the social distance is greater. It is argued that less social distance will help L2 learning because it can help bring learners into contact with L1 speakers or the target language.

For example, people from the United States are culturally similar to Canadians, while U. S. natives and Chinese are, by parison, relatively dissimilar. We could say that the social distance of the latter case exceed the former.

101   Sociocultural awareness***

the use of **role-play** in ESL classrooms as a means of helping students to overcome cultural "fatigue" while engaging in oral communication

Readings, films, simulation games, cultural assimilators, "culture capsules" and "culturgrams" [sic] are also available to language teachers to assist students in the process of *sociocultural awareness* in the classroom.

102   Sociopragmatics***

(a) the interface between pragmatics and social organization
(b) the <u>social perceptions underlying participants' interpretation and performance of communicative action</u>, which include the perception of relative power, social distance and degree of imposition (Brown and Levinson, 1987) as well as knowledge of mutual rights and obligations, taboos and conventional procedures (Thomas, 1983)

Ex

* **2024 기출 illocutionary force 예문**
American: what an unusual necklace. It's beautiful!
Samoan: Please take it.
The nonnative English speaker misunderstood the **illocutionary force** (intended meaning) of the utterance within the context.
In the Samoan culture, if one receives complement about something, it is the <u>cultural norm</u> to give it as a present. The American's compliment leads to a result that was not expected.

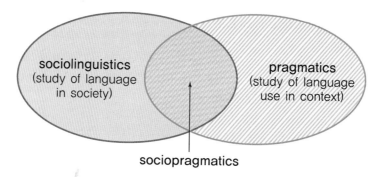

sociopragmatics

103   Speech acts***

(social interaction) one of the abilities enabling social interaction, using appropriate forms to accomplish such purposes as requesting, answering, greeting, agreeing, disagreeing, etc.

Three different meanings, or "forces", of speech acts
① **Locutionary** meaning: The basic literal or propositional meaning of an utterance (or written text) that is conveyed by its words and structures.
② **Illocutionary** force: The intended effect that an utterance or text has on the hearer or reader. (sender의 의도와 hearer의 이해는 다를 수 있다.)
③ **Perlocutionary** force: The actual effect the utterance has on the hearer. (결과 포함)

104 Spiral learning***

(a) a teaching method based on the premise that a learner learns more about a subject each time the topic is reviewed or encountered. The idea is that each time a learner encounters the topic, the student expands their knowledge or improves their skill level.
(b) a technique often used in education where the initial focus of instruction is the basic facts of a subject, with further details being introduced as learning progresses. Throughout instruction, both the initial basic facts and the relationships to later details are repeatedly emphasized to help enter into long-term memory.

Key principles of a spiral curriculum
* Topics are revisited.
* Levels of difficulty increase.
* New learning is related to previous learning.

105 Strategies-based Instruction (SBI)***

teacher learners with an emphasis on the strategic options that are available for learning; usually implying the teacher's facilitating awareness of those options in the learner and encouraging strategic action

106 Structural syllabus***

a language course that attends primarily to forms (grammar, phonology, lexicon) as organizing elements of a foreign language curriculum, as opposed to a functional syllabus

107   Subject-integrated class***

see **Content-based instruction**

108   Subjective needs***

Subjective needs focus on needs as seen through the eyes of the learners themselves. Sometimes, learners' perceived needs do not match their actual needs. For example, students of ten feel they should spend lots of time studying grammar in a class, when in reality they may need more time in communicative activities. Subjective needs are more difficult to gather, but are typically sought through interviews, questionnaires, teachers' perceptions, observations, and the opinions of "experts".
* learners' attitudes toward the target language, culture
* expectations that students have of themselves, and of the course
* purposes that students perceive for studying English
* specific language skills that students wish to focus on
* preferences (styles, strategies) that students have about their learning

109   Sustained Deep Learning (SDL)***

(a) the kind of learning that requires an extended period of time to achieve goals
(b) Schymann (1999)'s explanation of the neurobiological bases of motivation
(c) Looking at motivation as a powerful affective factor

In the case of complex fields of knowledge or skill "sustained deep learning" is needed. Sustained deep learning can happen even if the learner is forced to learn a specific type of knowledge or skill (as in a compulsory subject at school), but for the learning to be deep enough to be considered successfully accomplished, the learner must "pursue it to a higher degree", that is to say external achievement must be internalized, and motivation generated.

110 Syllabus [ⓑ]

a curriculum; also specifications of topics, forms, assignments, and schedules for completion of a course

111 Tactics [ⓑ]

specific manifestations or techniques within a metastrategy (or category of strategy) by a learner in a given setting for a particular purpose

112 Target task(s)***

uses of language in the world beyond the classroom that become the focus of classroom instruction
Target tasks refer to doing something outside the classroom and in the real world.

113 Task-based Language Teaching (TBLT)***

TBLT, an approach to language instruction that focuses on tasks
① Task: a classroom activity in which meaning is primary, there is a problem to solve, a relationship to real-world activities, and an objective that can be assessed in terms of an outcome
② Target task: It uses language in the world beyond the classroom that becomes the focus of classroom instruction. (David Nunan): [A task is] a piece of work undertaken for oneself or for others, freely or for some reward. Thus, examples of tasks include painting a fence, dressing a child, filling out forms, buying a pair of shoes, making an airline reservation, borrowing a library book, taking a driving test, typing a letter, weighing a patient, sorting letters, making a hotel reservation, writing a cheque, finding street destination, and helping someone across a road. In other words, by 'task' is meant the hundred and one things people do in everyday life, at work, at play and in between.

③ Pedagogical tasks: any of a sequence of techniques designed ultimately to teach students to perform the target task

Pedagogical tasks describe what learners do in the classroom to activate and develop their language skills. Although these tasks are designed for the classroom, there should also be a connection to corresponding real-world or target tasks. It is particularly important that the students are able to see a connection between the work they do in the classroom, and the world beyond the classroom.

④ Climactic pedagogical task (=ultimate task): The climactic pedagogical task actually involves students in some form of simulation of the target itself. (through a role play or a simulation)

114 Teachability hypothesis***

Manfred Pienemann proposed that in order for linguistic structures to be learned, they must be relatively close to a learner's current interlanguage status. Structures they are too far beyond the learner's interlanguage are not teachable. Thus, he argued that the linguistic structures that are taught in the L2 classroom should follow the learner's stages of acquisition. However, there are some difficulties with such a proposal: (a) the stages of acquisition are known for only a limited number of linguistic structures in only a few languages (b) learners within the same class may be at different stages of acquisition.

115 Teacher-centered instruction***

The teacher controls everything; students speak only when asked to; the teacher is an authority who is not to be questioned.

116 Teaching styles ©

particular preferences of a teacher's performance that reflects his or her personality, values, and beliefs and that can vary greatly from individual to individual

117　Teacher's roles (From the most directive role to less directive)***

① Controller: The teacher determines what the students do, when they should speak, and what language forms they should use.
② Director: The teacher is like a conductor of an orchestra or a director of a drama.
③ Manager: The teacher plans lessons, modules, and courses.
④ Facilitator: The teacher facilitates the process of learning, of making learning easier for students.
⑤ Resource: The teacher is available for advice and counsel when the students seek it.

118　Technique(s) Ⓔ

any of a wide variety of exercises, activities, procedures, or tasks used in the language classroom for realizing lesson objectives

119　Terminal objective Ⓔ

final learning outcome

120　Textbook adaptation***

① adding: It means to add necessary materials by expanding or extending.
② deleting: It refers to omission of some exercises quantitatively by answering a proportion of it or qualitatively by omitting a tedious and boring exercise.
③ modifying: It can involve rewriting to change the content, or restructuring to change the way the task is carried out in class; for example an individual writing task could be restructured as a group activity.
(Modification is a very general term in the language applying to any kind of change. In other words, the act or process of changing something in order to improve it or make it more acceptable is known as modification or rewriting. Rewriting, therefore, may relate activities more closely to learners' own backgrounds and interests, introduce models of authentic language, or set more purposeful, problem solving tasks where the answers are not always known before the teacher asks the question.)

④ simplifying: It is rewording or paraphrasing the text with out damaging its authenticity. It usually involves adapting the language level of texts.
⑤ reordering: This procedure refers to the possibility of putting the parts of a course book in a different order. This may mean adjusting the sequence of presentation within a unit, or taking units in a different sequence from that originally intended.

121   Theme-based instruction***

an organizing framework for a language course that transcends formal or structural requirements in a curriculum and focuses on meaningful topics as organizing elements of units and lessons (see also **CBI**)

122   Think-aloud strategy / technique***

While modeling the think-aloud strategy "teachers verbalize aloud while reading a selection orally. Their verbalizations include describing things they're doing as they read to monitor their comprehension. The purpose of the think-aloud strategy is to model for students how skilled readers construct meaning from a text." (Farr, Connor, 2015).
Purpose: The purpose for using a think-aloud is to help students improve their comprehension.

123   Total Physical Response (TPR)***

Total Physical Response (TPR) is a method of teaching language or vocabulary concepts by using physical or kinesthetic movement accompanied by language practice. The process mimics the way that infants learn their first language, and it reduces student inhibitions and lowers stress. The method is an example of the comprehension approach to language teaching. Listening and responding (with actions) serves two purposes: It is a means of quickly recognizing meaning in the language being learned, and a means of passively learning the structure of the language itself. Grammar is not taught explicitly but can be learned from the language input. TPR is a valuable way to learn vocabulary, especially idiomatic terms, (**Ex** phrasal verbs.)

124 Translanguaging***

(a) a classroom manifestation to implement flexible multilingualism
(b) code-switching or translating in reading, writing, discussing, note-taking, or singing
(a) a strategy in which bilingual students and teachers engage in multiple discursive practices in order to make sense of meanings and functions of target forms

03

125 Uncertainty avoidance***

(a) the extent to which people within a culture are uncomfortable with situations they perceive as unstructured, unclear, or unpredictable; cultural ambiguity intolerance
(b) Strong uncertainty avoidance implies a need for security, strict rules, and absolute truths.
(c) one of cultural dimensions that helps people understand what holds communities together

126 World Englishes***

varieties of English spoken and written in many different countries, especially those not in the traditional "*inner circle*" (countries traiditionally considered to be dominated by native speakers of English, **Ex** the UK, US, Australia, New Zealand...) vs *outer circle* (countries that use English as a common lingua franca and in which English is for many people nativized, **Ex** India, Singapore, the Philippines...).

※ Read the following descriptions and fill in the blanks.

01 _____

cultural adaptation
John Schumann's THIS model states that some L2 learners do not progress beyond the early stages of linguistic acquisition with a target language because of social and psychological distance between the speaker's culture and the target culture. A lack of THIS or cultural adaptation, according to the model, can lead to linguistic fossilization or pidginization. (Ellis)

02 _____ _____ **(of content-based language teaching)**

linking subject-matter teachers and language teachers in content-based courses affect emotion or feeling

03 _____

(특히, 비언어적 의사소통의 상황에서) external factors of a person, such as clothing and ornamentation, and their effect on communication

04 _____

individual effort and action through which learners initiate language, problem solving, strategic action, and the generation of linguistic input

05 _____ _____

THIS involves <u>online and face-to-face instruction</u>. Both are used <u>alongside each other</u> in order to provide a comprehensive learning experience. For example, a trainer might give learners a list of online resources they can use to broaden their understanding of the topic, or ask them to complete an online group project that centers on a subject they are currently discussing. In the case of THIS, <u>online materials do not take the place of face-to-face instruction</u>; <u>instead, the two modalities complement one another.</u>

06 _____ _____   **(Canale and Swain, 1983)**

a term used to refer to a <u>learner's ability to use language</u>
The term, popularized in SLA, refers to learners' language knowledge that includes more than just grammatical accuracy or an idealized competence in the language. THIS is seen as being composed of several difference components: linguistic competence, sociolinguistic competence, discourse competence, strategic competence.

① **Grammatical competence:** Knowledge of lexical items and of rules of morphology, syntax, sentence-grammar semantics, and phonology. It is the competence we associate with <u>mastering the linguistic code of a language</u>, the **linguistic competence** referred to by Hymes (1972) and Paulston (1974)

② **Sociolinguistic competence:** The ability to follow <u>sociocultural rules</u> of language. This requires an understanding of the social context in which language is used: <u>the roles of the participants, the information they share, and the function of the interaction.</u>

③ **Discourse competence:** The ability to connect sentences in stretches of discourse and to form a meaningful whole out of a series of utterances. With its <u>inter-sentential relationships</u>, discourse encompasses everything <u>from simple spoken conversations to lengthy written texts</u> (articles, books, etc)

④ **Strategic competence:** The ability to use verbal and nonverbal communicative techniques to <u>compensate for breakdowns in communication or insufficient competence</u>. It includes the ability to make "<u>repairs</u>" and to sustain communication through <u>paraphrase, circumlocution, repetition, avoidance, and guessing.</u>

07 _____ _____ **(Littlewood, 2011)**

① **Linguistic competence** (=grammatical competence)
② **Discourse competence** (=textual competence)
③ **Pragmatic competence** (=strategic competence): the ability to use linguistic resources to convey and interpret meanings in real situations, including those where learners encounter problems due to gaps in their knowledge.
④ **Sociolinguistic competence** (same as Canale and Swain's definition)
⑤ **Sociocultural competence:** cultural knowledge and assumptions that affect the exchange of meanings

08 _____ **activities**

activities in which you ask your students to derive some information from that which you give them. They are required to comprehend and convey information, much as in an information gap activity, but the information that they are asked to convey is not exactly the same that they comprehend. They are asked to use reason and logic to decide what information to convey and what resolution to make for the problem at hand. For example, you might ask your students to make a decision between speed and cost or cost and quality, given a certain situation and various constraints.

09 _____ _____ **(=tailored testing)**

THIS is a form of computer-based test that adapts to the examinee's ability level. For this reason, it has also been called tailored testing. In other words, it is a form of computer-administered test in which the next item or set of items selected to be administered depends on the correctness of the test taker's responses to the most recent items administered.

10 _____

searching for words in context and collocations
Indexing of words that enables one to reference words in the multiple possible contexts in which they appear in spoken or written language.

11 _____ _____

in the process of acculturation, phenomena involving mild irritability, depression, anger, or possibly deep psychological crisis due to the foreignness of the new cultural milieu
THIS is an experience a person may have when one moves to a cultural environment which is different from one's own; it is also the personal disorientation a person may feel when experiencing an unfamiliar way of life due to immigration or a visit to a new country, a move between social environments, or simply transition to another type of life. One of the most common causes of THIS involves individuals in a foreign environment. THIS can be described as consisting of at least one of four distinct phases: honeymoon, negotiation, adjustment, and adaptation.

12 _____ _____

It is the ability to understand and use information in multiple formats from a wide variety of sources when it is presented via computers. (Gilster)

13 _____ _____

the concept that when <u>learners are spurred to induce language</u>. or other content, as opposed to being told by the teacher, <u>greater retention</u> results.

14 _____ _____ **(debate)**

a term for a movement and philosophy in the US that seeks to make English the official language of the US and to discourage the use of bilingual education

15 _____ _____

instruction that highlights <u>giving students concrete experiences</u> in which they must use language in order to fulfill the objectives of a lesson
It is an engaged learning process whereby students "<u>learn by doing</u>" and by reflecting on the experience. This type of learning highlights giving learners <u>concrete experiences in which they must use language</u> in order to fulfill the objectives of a lesson. (Contextualize language, integrate skills, authentic purposes)

> **Ex**
>
> _hands on projects, field trips, research projects, creating a video_

16 _____ _____

It is a pedagogical model in which <u>the typical lecture and homework elements of a course are reversed</u>. THIS, which is also known as a flipped classroom, is a bit more clear-cut. There is a divide between the technology and face-to-face elements of the learning experience. A learner is asked to watch an e-Learning video or participate in another online learning exercise BEFORE coming to class. In the classroom the new materials are explored at-length. In most cases, the knowledge that is learned online is applied in the classroom.

17 _____

educational model that typically provides the majority of subject-matter content through the medium of the L2 (see also **CBI**)

18 _____ _____

model of education with a focus on learners' needs and goals and individual differences in a supportive atmosphere that offers students choices and some control

19 _____ _____

A view that lexis and grammar are two inherently connected parts of a single entity and should not be treated separately "Vocabulary and grammatical structures are interdependent; so much so that it is possible to say with some justification that words have their own grammar." This interdependency of lexis and grammar is evident everywhere in language. For example, lexical verbs have valency (v+sth) patterns: some verbs can be used with a direct object, or with both a direct object and an indirect object, others need no object at all.

20 _____

the language that is used to talk about language
It may consist of both technical or non-technical terms. Examples of technical metalinguistic terms in SLA would be present perfect tense and subject verb agreement. Examples of non-technical metalinguistic terms would include word and sentence.

21 _____ _____

: a language teaching method that simulates child language acquisition by emphasizing communication, comprehensible input, kinesthetic activities, and virtually no grammatical analysis (also natural method)

: a term for a number of language-teaching methods which were developed in the nineteenth century as a reaction to the grammar translation method

These methods emphasized:

(a) the use of the spoken language

(b) the use of objects and actions in teaching the meanings of words and structures

(c) the need to make language teaching follow the natural principles of first language learning

THIS aims to develop communicative skills, and it is primarily intended to be used with beginning learners. It is presented as a set of principles that can apply to a wide range of learners and teaching situations, and concrete objectives depend on the specific context in which it is used. Terrell outlines three basic principles of the approach:

"Focus of instruction is on communication rather than its form."

"Speech production comes slowly and is never forced."

"Early speech goes through natural stages. (yes or no response, one-word answers, lists of words, short phrases, complete sentences)"

22 _____ _____ / _____ _____

THIS is the process of specifying the learners' language needs in advance of designing a course of them. The analysis can then be used to materials, and also the methodology. Finally, the needs analysis can be used in the design of assessment and evaluation procedures.

THIS refers to a systematic process for determining and addressing needs, overall purposes of the course, or "gaps" that the course is intended to fill, and the opinions of both course designers and students about their reasons for developing/taking the course.
It is important to identify at least two types of needs: **objective** and **subjective**

03

23 _____ _____

any of a sequence of techniques designed ultimately to teach students to perform the target task

24 _____ _____

the syllabus focusing on the skills and processes involved in learning language
(Ex task-based syllabus, learner-centered syllabus, content syllabus)

25 _____ _____

the syllabus focusing on things learned at the end of the learning process/ outcomes
(Ex structural syllabus, situational syllabus, notional-functional syllabus)

26 _____

THIS in EFL terms refers to any real objects we use in the classroom to bring the class to life. (usually for teaching vocabulary)

27 _____ _____ (= _____ _____)

the deliberate separation of L2 students from native speakers of the target
language for the purpose of content instruction (see also **CBI**)

28 _____ _____

a language course that attends <u>primarily to forms</u> (grammar, phonology, lexicon)
as organizing elements of a foreign language curriculum, as opposed to a
functional syllabus

29 _____ _____

THIS type of tasks use language in the world beyond the classroom that becomes
the focus of classroom instruction
THIS refer to doing something outside the classroom and in the real world.

30 _____ _____

an organizing framework for a language course that transcends formal or
structural requirements in a curriculum and focuses on <u>meaningful topics as
organizing elements of units and lessons</u> (see also **CBI**)

31 _____ **strategy / technique**

While modeling the strategy, "teachers verbalize aloud while reading a selection orally. Their verbalizations include describing things they're doing as they read to monitor their comprehension. The purpose of THIS is to model for students how skilled readers construct meaning from a text." (Farr, Connor, 2015).
Purpose: The purpose for using THIS is to help students improve their comprehension.

32 _____ _____

varieties of English spoken and written in many different countries, especially those not in the traditional "inner circle" (countries traiditionally considered to be dominated by native speakers of English, **Ex** the UK, US, Australia, New Zealand...) vs outer circle (countries that use English as a c ommon lingua franca and in which English is for many peple nativized, **Ex** India, Singapore, the Philippines...).

Answers

01 Acculturation

02 Adjunct model

03 Artifact

04 Autonomy

05 Blended learning

06 Communicative competence

07 Communicative competence

08 Reasoning-gap

09 Computer-adaptive testing

10 Concordancing

11 Culture shock

12 Digital literacy

13 Discovery learning

14 English only (debate)

15 Experiential learning

16 Flipped learning

17 Immersion

18 Learner-centered instruction

19 Lexico-grammatical approach

20 Metalanguage

21 Natural approach / Needs assessment

22 Needs analysis

23 Pedagogical tasks (=pedagogic tasks)

24 Process-oriented syllabus

25 Product-oriented syllabus

26 Realia

27 Sheltered model (Sheltered-language instruction)

28 Structural syllabus

29 Target tasks

30 Theme-based instruction

31 Think-aloud

32 Word Englishes

Note

Listening

※ **Review the following Key Terms list and put a checkmark next to Terms that you do not know the exact meaning.**

☐ Bottom-up processing

☐ Contextual knowledge

☐ Chunking / Clustering

☐ Dialogue

☐ Dictogloss

☐ Extensive listening

☐ Inferential listening

☐ Information transfer

☐ Intensive listening

☐ Interpersonal dialogue

☐ Jigsaw listening

☐ Listening for details

☐ Listening for gist

☐ Monitoring

☐ Monologue

☐ Predicting

☐ Reduced forms

☐ Redundancy

☐ Scanning

☐ Transactional dialogue

☐ Top-down processing

01   Bottom-up processing***

a type or cognitive activity that involves learners in the process of recognizing and decoding the individual components of language in order to comprehend a sentence or utterance

02   Chunk / Chunking (clustering)***

(a) the act of combining words together as a phrase to seamlessly connect them
(b) Chunking helps your spoken language flow smoothly without having a staggered or choppy rhythm. Or, in teaching listening, you need to help students to pick out manageable clusters of words.
(c) one characteristic of spoken language that can make listening difficult for second language learners
(d) Sometimes second language learners will try to retain overly long constituents (a whole sentence or even several sentences), or they will err in the other direction in trying to attend to every word in an utterance.

03   Contextual knowledge***

For receptive skills, prior and shared knowledge involve both *schematic* and *contextual knowledge*. *Schematic knowledge* consists of both *content schemata* and *formal schemata*.
(related to listening) listener's overall sense of the situation regarding the participants, the setting, the topic and the purpose
(related to reading) readers should consider the title and subtitles of the text, the author's background, and the larger context in which the text appeared.

04 Dialogue ®

one type of spoken language
It involves two or more speakers and can be subdivided into those exchanges that promote social relationships (**interpersonal**) and those for which the purpose is to convey propositional or factual information (**transactional**). In each case, participants may have a good deal of shared knowledge (background knowledge, schemata); therefore, the *familiarity* of *the interlocutors* will produce conversations with more assumptions, implications, and other meanings hidden between the lines.

05 Dictogloss***

a type of classroom activity in which learners take notes while listening to a short L2 passage
Learners are subsequently asked to reconstruct the passage. The primary aim of the activity is for learners to notice gaps in their L2 grammar and vocabulary knowledge as they work on the reconstruction.

> **Ex**
>
> Learners discuss the sea. The teacher then explains the task, and reads a short text on the sea to the class, who just listens. The teacher reads the text again, and the learners take notes. In groups, the learners then reconstruct the text.

06 Extensive listening (listening for pleasure)***

all types of listening activities that allow learners to receive a lot of comprehensible and enjoyable listening input
These activities can be teacher-directed dictations or read-alouds or self-directed listening for pleasure that can be done outside the classroom. The key consideration here is that learners get to do a lot of meaningful listening practice.

07   Inferential listening***

the type of listening we do when we wish to know how the speaker feels. It may involve inferring.

08   Information transfer***

This activity involves getting students to put spoken or written texts into another form, such as a chart, grid, picture, table or diagram – or vice-versa. Make sure that the students can't just copy chunks without understanding them by requiring a different organization to the text. These tasks encourage deep processing of information. The interpretation of text, diagram or tables is a skill that is very useful both in academic and everyday life.

09   Intensive listening (listening for a purpose)***

Use taped material. Most course books include tapes and many teachers rely on them to provide their students; with a good listening course. Intensive listening is crucial to help students develop effective listening strategies and build *bottom-up listening skills*, in addition to the *top-down skills* that are emphasized in global listening activities.

10   Interpersonal dialogue***

two or more speakers' exchanges to promote social relationships (social type, person-oriented) (see also **transactional dialogue**)

11　Jigsaw listening***

In this activity, three different audio clips containing different perspectives are prepared, for example, one containing an interview with someone who has witnessed an accident, one interviewing someone who has seen a UFO, and one about someone who has been involved in a natural catastrophe. Then the class is divided into three groups: Group A, B, and C. Each group goes into a different part of the room and listens to its part of the interview. Each group completes a task (answering comprehension questions, filling in a chart, etc.) Next, new groups are formed, each containing one student from groups A, B, and C. The three students in each new group now report what they heard or role-play the person describing the scene. As a group, the students then decide who the most reliable witness is.

12　Listening for details***

When we <u>cannot afford to ignore anything</u> because we don't know what kind of information we need.

13　Listening for gist***

This refers to <u>the general idea</u> of what is being said, as well as who is speaking to whom and why, and how successful they are in communicating their point.

14　Monitoring***

This is used to confirm predictions made during pre-listening.

15 Monologue [Ⓑ]

one type of spoken language
When one speaker uses spoken language for any length of time, as in speeches, lectures, readings, news broadcasts, etc, the hearer must process long stretches of speech without interruption - the stream of speech will go on whether or not the hearer comprehends. (see also **dialogues**)
① planned / rehearsed / spoken from a written text or notes
② spontaneous / impromptu / unplanned

04

16 Predicting***

This is for generating the learners' schemata. Pre-listening tasks serve to get the learners to think about and talk about the content of what they are about to hear.

17 Reduced forms***

(related to listening skills) Spoken language has many reduced forms and sentence fragments. Reduction can be phonological ("Djeetyet?" for "Did you eat yet?"), morphological (contractions like "I'll"), syntactic (elliptical forms like "When will you be back?" "Tomorrow, maybe.") or pragmatic (phone rings in a house, child answers and yells to another room in the house, "Mom! Phone!"). These reductions pose significant difficulties for second language learners.
(related to speaking skills) Contractions, elisions, reduced vowels, and other similar characteristics all pose special problems in teaching spoken English. Students who don't learn colloquial contractions can sometimes develop a stilted, bookish quality of speaking.

18 Redundancy***

information that is expressed more than once
rephrasings, repetitions, elaborations, and litter insertions of "I mean" and "you know"
in spoken language
Such redundancy helps the hearer to process meaning by offering more time and extra information.

19 Scanning***

When we don't need to understand everything, but only a very specific part.

20 Top-down processing***

This term refers to a type of cognitive process is which learners draw on their general knowledge and world experiences in order to help them understand the language they encounter

21 Transactional dialogue***

Two or more speakers' exchanges to convey propositional or factual information.

※ **Read the following descriptions and fill in the blanks.**

01 _____ _____

a type or cognitive activity that involves learners in the process of recognizing and decoding the individual components of language in order to comprehend a sentence or utterance

02 _____

a type of classroom activity in which learners take notes while listening to a short L2 passage
Learners are subsequently asked to reconstruct the passage. The primary aim of the activity is for learners to notice gaps in their L2 grammar and vocabulary knowledge as they work on the reconstruction.

> **Ex**
> Learners discuss the sea. The teacher then explains the task, and reads a short text on the sea to the class, who just listens. The teacher reads the text again, and the learners take notes. In groups, the learners then reconstruct the text.

03 _____ _____ **(listening for pleasure)**

all types of listening activities that allow learners to receive a lot of comprehensible and enjoyable listening input
These activities can be teacher-directed dictations or read-alouds or self-directed listening for pleasure that can be done outside the classroom. The key consideration here is that learners get to do a lot of meaningful listening practice.

04 _____ _____

the type of listening we do when we wish to know how the speaker feels. It may involve inferring.

05 _____ _____

This activity involves getting students to <u>put spoken or written texts into another form,</u> such as a chart, grid, picture, table or diagram – or vice-versa. Make sure that the students <u>can't just copy</u> chunks without understanding them by requiring a different organization to the text. These tasks encourage <u>deep processing</u> of information. The interpretation of text, diagram or tables is a skill that is very useful both in academic and everyday life.

06 _____ _____ **(listening for a purpose)**

Use taped material. Most <u>course books</u> include tapes and many teachers rely on them to provide their students; with <u>a good listening course.</u> THIS is crucial to <u>help students develop effective listening strategies</u> and build *bottom-up listening skills,* in addition <u>to the *top-down skills*</u> that are emphasized in global listening activities.

07 _____ _____

two or more speakers' exchanges to promote <u>social relationships.</u> (social type, person-oriented) (see also **transactional dialogue**)

08 _____ _____ _____

When we <u>cannot afford to ignore anything</u> because we don't know what kind of information we need.

09 _____ _____ _____

This refers to the general idea of what is being said, as well as who is speaking to whom and why, and how successful they are in communicating their point.

10 _____

This is used to confirm predictions made during pre-listening.

11 _____

This is for generating the learners' schemata. Pre-listening tasks serve to get the learners to think about and talk about the content of what they are about to hear.

12 _____

When we don't need to understand everything, but only a very specific part.

13 _____ _____

This term refers to a type of cognitive process is which learners draw on their general knowledge and world experiences in order to help them understand the language they encounter.

14 _____ _____

Two or more speakers' exchanges to convey propositional or factual information.

Answers

01 Bottom-up processing

02 Dictogloss

03 Extensive listening

04 Inferential listening

05 Information transfer

06 Intensive listening

07 Interpersonal dialogue

08 Listening for details

09 Listening for gist

10 Monitoring

11 Predicting

12 Scanning

13 Top-down processing

14 Transactional dialogue

Chapter

05

Reading

※ **Review the following Key Terms list and put a checkmark next to Terms that you do not know the exact meaning.**

☐　Advance organizer

☐　Authentic language

☐　Basal readers (Basal approach, Bottom-up)

☐　Bottom-up (data-driven) processing

☐　Content schemata

☐　Contextual knowledge

☐　Discourse markers

☐　Exploitability

☐　Extensive reading

☐　Formal schemata

☐　Graded readers

☐　Graphic Organizer (GO)

☐　Guessing

☐　Inferencing

☐　Intensive reading

☐　Interactive processing

☐　Language Experience Approach (LEA, 1967) (Top-down)

☐　Linguistic approach (Bottom-up)

☐　Literature-based approach (Top-down)

☐　Phonics approach (Bottom-up)

☐　Readability

☐　Scanning

☐　Schema theory

☐　Schemata

☐　Semantic mapping / Clustering

	Skimming
☐	SQ3R
☐	Suitability of content
☐	Top-down (concept-driven) processing

01   Advance organizer***

making a general but comprehensive preview of the organizing concept or principle in an anticipated learning activity

It is relevant introductory materials presented in advance in any format of text, graphics, or hypermedia. Instructors may use an advance organizer to present a framework for module content. The aim of this is to relate what a student already knows to the new content to be learned and thus increase retention. Advance organizers should be at a higher level of abstraction, generality, and inclusiveness than the content to be presented.

02   Authentic language ®

the language used in real life by real language users, (particularly L1 speakers) and unmodified for L2 learner convenience

It can be seen as being relevant to learners because it is real and potentially interesting. In addition, it is the type of language that many learners ultimately aspire to comprehend. However, authentic language may also be too advanced or difficult for learners. Consequently, input in the L2 classroom may need to be modified in some way, especially for lower proficiency learners.

03   Basal readers (Basal approach, Bottom-up)***

These are textbooks used to teach reading and associated skills to school children. A standard basal series comes with individual identical books for students, a Teacher's edition of the book, and a collection of workbooks, assessments, and activities. (compared to **graded readers**)

04   Bottom-up (data-driven) processing***

The meaning of any text must be "decoded" by the reader and that students are "reading" when they can "sound out" words on a page.
(related to reading skills)
Readers must first recognize a multiplicity of linguistic signals (letters, morphemes, syllables words, phrases, grammatical cues, discourse markers) and use their linguistic data-processing mechanisms to impose some sort of order on these signals. These data-driven operations obviously require a sophisticated knowledge of the language itself.

05

05   Content schemata***

include what we know about people, the world, culture, and the universe

06   Contextual knowledge***

For receptive skills, prior and shared knowledge involve both *schematic* and *contextual knowledge*. *Schematic knowledge* consists of both *content schemata* and *formal schemata*.
(related to listening) listener's overall sense of the situation regarding the participants, the setting, the topic and the purpose
(related to reading) readers should consider the title and subtitles of the text, the author's background, and the larger context in which the text appeared.

07   Discourse markers***

sequentially dependent elements which bracket units of talk
Sometimes called discourse particles or pragmatic markers, the term is often used to refer to words or phrases that appear to have no grammatical or semantic function, such as you know, like, oh, well, I mean, actually, basically, OK as well as connectives like because, so, and, but and or.

Two functional classes of discourse markers:

(a) local markers: mark micro structures within a single topic (**Ex** I mean)

(b) global markers: can be used to signpost transition from one topic to another

(**Ex** anyway)

Discourse markers signal relationships among ideas as expressed through phrases, clauses, and sentences. A clear comprehension of such markers can greatly enhance learners' reading efficiency.

> **Ex**
>
> *** Categories: markers**
> · Enumerative: first(ly), second(ly), third(ly), one, two, three...
> · Additive: again, then again, also, moreover, equally, similarly, by the way, incidentally...
> · Logical sequence: so far, altogether, therefore, to sum up, as a result, now, to summarize...
> · Explicative: namely, in other words, better, rather, by this we mean...
> · Illustrative: for example, for instance...
> · Contrastive: alternatively, or rather, but then, instead, by contrast, however, nevertheless, for all that, in spite of, at the same time...

The concept of discourse markers can be expanded to refer to nonlinguistic phenomena. For example, in speech, a rise in pitch could be used to mark the start of a new topic. In writing, discourse can be organized with visual elements like paragraph spaces, subheadings, etc.

08   Exploitability (for choosing reading texts)***

It refers to how the text can be used to develop the students' competence as readers. A text that can not be exploited for teaching purposes has no use in the classroom. Just because it is in English does not mean that it can be useful.

a text that facilitates the achievement of certain language and content goals, that is exploitable for instructional tasks and techniques, and that is integratable with other skills (listening, speaking, writing)

09　Extensive reading***

Readers spend as much time as possible on reading for pleasure or general language improvement, mostly in real-life situations. Readers choose the text for themselves and tend to read it fast. The materials for extensive reading should be at least 98% comprehensible to the students.

10　Formal schemata***

(a) consist of our knowledge about language and discourse structure
(b) knowledge of how discourse is organized with respect to different genres, topics or purposes

11　Graded reader(s)***

A graded reader is an "easy reading" book that supports the extensive reading approach to teaching English as a second or foreign language. Graded readers can be adapted from literacy classics, films, biographies, travel books, etc., or they can be original works written at a less demanding language level. Although they employ simplified language, graded readers do not necessarily lack narrative depth or avoid complex themes; often they cover the same range of "series" themes as books written for native speaker audiences.

12　Graphic Organizer (GO)***

(a) (a supplementary tool in while & post activities) a pedagogical tool that uses visual symbols to express knowledge and concepts through relationship between them
(b) a specific type of advance organizer and are usually applied to listening and reading comprehension pre-task activities

The idea is that access to the text will be facilitated if the listener or reader prepares their mind (more specifically their schema) before being faced with the text. This can be achieved by the teacher presenting a 'concept map' (words connected in meaning radiating out from a central word) or by the teacher conducting an initial elicitation activity, producing a graph on the board in the middle of which is the central core word (Ex famine) and from which a mind-map is formed linking all possible connecting words to it. (Ex hunger, starvation, poverty, drought) This activation of schema is said to allow the student to predict what words are likely to occur in the text and therefore reduce the cognitive load by, as it were, having done some of the comprehension beforehand, or by regrouping the INPUT into more manageable chunks.

13   Guessing★★☆

When the reader tries to figure out the meaning of an unknown word, s/he uses the text surrounding that word – the context – to provide him/her with clues

14   Inferencing★★★

the process of putting pieces of information together
In other words, when the reader "infers" something, she is drawing an unstated conclusion from the information that s/he already has.

15   Intensive reading★★☆

usually a classroom-oriented activity in which students focus on the linguistic or semantic details of a passage

16 Interactive processing***

Reading here is the process of combining textual information with the information the reader brings to a text. The processing involves what is on the written page and what a reader brings to it using both skills. Reading is seen as the interaction between reader and text.

17 Language Experience Approach (LEA, 1967) (Top-down)***

An integrated-skills approach initially used in teaching native language reading skills, but more recently adapted to second language learning contexts.
(a) a specialized form of experiential learning
(b) Students' personal experiences (a trip to the zoo, a movie, a family gathering at a park) are used as the basis for discussion, and then students, with the help of the teacher, write about the "experience" which is preserved in the form of a "book".

* **Benefits**
  ① intrinsic involvement of students in creating their own stories
  ② Students are directly involved in the creative process of fashioning their own products.
  ③ All four skills are readily implied in carrying out a project.

18 Linguistic approach (Bottom-up)***

It is based upon the tenets of *structural linguists*. Those who advocate this particular approach are generally concerned with helping students internalize regular patterns of spelling/sound correspondence, on the assumption that this will enable them to read unfamiliar words without actually stopping to sound them out.
(직접적으로 phonics를 가르치기보다 letters/sound pattern에 많이 노출시켜 자연스럽게 책을 읽을 수 있게 하는 것이 목적 **Ex** ay, ey, oo, oe, etc.)

19 Literature-based approach (Top-down)***

It uses literary selections as major instructional materials that can be tailored to students' interests and needs. In this approach, students can better focus on meaning while reading for their interest and enjoyment. (좋은 문학작품을 읽은 후, 토론이나 글쓰기 진행)

20 Phonics approach (Bottom-up) ⑤

It helps students learn letter/sound correspondences so that they can sound out, or "decode," words. Often, they are taught not only basic letter/sound correspondences but rules for pronouncing letters and combinations of letters and for sounding out words. Emphasis on phonics is typically part of "reading readiness" programs.

21 Readability (for choosing reading texts)***

It is used to describe the combination of the structural and lexical difficulty of a text, as well as referring to the amount of new vocabulary and any new grammatical forms present. It is important to assess the right level for the right student.
a text with lexical and structural difficulty that will challenge students without overwhelming them

22 Scanning***

quickly searching for a particular piece or pieces of information in a text
The reader has a question in mind and does not read every word, only key words that will answer the question.

23 Schema theory***

the concept that information is <u>stored in long-term memory</u> in <u>networks</u> of connected facts, concepts, and structures, which learners bring to bear on comprehension and production of language

24 Schemata***

background information that a language user brings to bear on a text

25 Semantic mapping / Clustering***

grouping ideas into meaningful/semantic clusters to help readers provide some order to a long string of ideas or events from a text
The idea of use this tool is <u>to organize the main ideas of the topic</u> what they are reading. This can be done individually, but it is useful as a productive group work technique as students collectively <u>induce order and hierarchy to a passage</u>.

26 Skimming***

It is a high-speed reading technique that can save the reader time and help him/her get through a text quickly. The reader gets <u>the general sense of a passage (gist)</u>, not specific details.

27 SQ3R***

a pedagogical set of procedures for approaching a reading text involving (in sequential order): *survey, question, read, recite, review* strategic investment a certain degree of investment of one's time and effort into using effective strategies for accomplishing L2 goals.

① Survey: skim the text for an overview of main ideas (also through titles, pictures, etc)
② Question: The reader asks questions about what he or she wishes to get out of the text.
③ Read: read the text while looking for answers to the previously formulated questions
④ Recite: reprocess the salient points of the text through oral and written language
⑤ Review: assess the importance of what one has just read and incorporate it into long-term associations

28 Suitability of content (for choosing reading texts)***

Among the three main criteria when choosing texts, it can be considered to be the most important, in that the reading material should interest the students as well as be relevant to their needs. The texts should motivate as well as.

material that students will find interesting, enjoyable, challenging, and appropriate for their goals in learning English

29 Top-down (concept-driven) processing***

By using this processing, readers bring meaning to text based on their experiential background and interpret text based on their prior knowledge.
(related to reading skills)
conceptually driven processing in which we draw on our own intelligence and experience to understand a text

※ **Read the following descriptions and fill in the blanks.**

01 _____ _____

the language used in real life by real language users, (particularly L1 speakers) and unmodified for L2 learner convenience

It can be seen as being relevant to learners because it is real and potentially interesting. In addition, it is the type of language that many learners ultimately aspire to comprehend. However, THIS may also be too advanced or difficult for learners. Consequently, input in the L2 classroom may need to be modified in some way, especially for lower proficiency learners.

02 _____ _____

These are textbooks used to teach reading and associated skills to school children. A standard basal series comes with individual identical books for students, a Teacher's edition of the book, and a collection of workbooks, assessments, and activities.

(compared to **graded readers**)

03 _____ _____

The meaning of any text must be "decoded" by the reader and that students are "reading" when they can "sound out" words on a page.

(related to reading skills)

Readers must first recognize a multiplicity of linguistic signals (letters, morphemes, syllables words, phrases, grammatical cues, discourse markers) and use their linguistic data-processing mechanisms to impose some sort of order on these signals. These data-driven operations obviously require a sophisticated knowledge of the language itself.

04 _____ _____

include what we know about people, the world, culture, and the universe

05 _____ **(for choosing reading texts)**

It refers to how the text can be used to develop the students' competence as readers. A text that can not be exploited for teaching purposes has no use in the classroom. Just because it is in English does not mean that it can be useful.
a text that facilitates the achievement of certain language and content goals, that is exploitable for instructional tasks and techniques, and that is integratable with other skills (listening, speaking, writing)

06 _____ _____

Readers spend as much time as possible on reading for pleasure or general language improvement, mostly in real-life situations. Readers choose the text for themselves and tend to read it fast. The materials for THIS should be at least 98% comprehensible to the students.

07 _____ _____

(a) consist of our knowledge about language and discourse structure
(b) knowledge of how discourse is organized with respect to different genres, topics or purposes

08 _____

When the reader tries to figure out the meaning of an unknown word, s/he uses the text surrounding that word – the context – to provide him/her with clues

09 _____

the process of putting pieces of information together
In other words, when the reader "infers" something, s/he is drawing an unstated conclusion from the information that s/he already has.

10 _____   _____

usually a classroom-oriented activity in which students focus on the linguistic or semantic details of a passage

11 _____   _____

Reading here is the process of combining textual information with the information the reader brings to a text. The processing involves what is on the written page and what a reader brings to it using both skills. Reading is seen as the interaction between reader and text.

12 _____   _____   **approach**

Students' personal experiences (a trip to the zoo, a movie, a family gathering at a park) are used as the basis for discussion, and then students, with the help of the teacher, write about the "experience" which is preserved in the form of a "book".

13 _____ **approach**

It is based upon the tenets of *structural linguists*. Those who advocate this particular approach are generally concerned with helping students internalize regular patterns of spelling/sound correspondence, on the assumption that this will enable them to read unfamiliar words without actually stopping to sound them out.

(직접적으로 phonics를 가르치기보다 letters/sound pattern에 많이 노출시켜 자연스럽게 책을 읽을 수 있게 하는 것이 목적 **Ex** ay, ey, oo, oe, etc.)

14 _____ **approach**

It uses literary selections as major instructional materials that can be tailored to students' interests and needs. In this approach, students can better focus on meaning while reading for their interest and enjoyment. (좋은 문학작품을 읽은 후, 토론이나 글쓰기 진행)

15 _____ **approach**

It helps students learn letter/sound correspondences so that they can sound out, or "decode," words. Often, they are taught not only basic letter/sound correspondences but rules for pronouncing letters and combinations of letters and for sounding out words. Emphasis on phonics is typically part of "reading readiness" programs.

16 _____ **(for choosing reading texts)**

It is used to describe the <u>combination of the structural and lexical difficulty</u> of a text, as well as referring to the amount of <u>new vocabulary and any new grammatical forms</u> present. It is important to assess the right level for the right student.

a text with lexical and structural difficulty that will challenge students without overwhelming them

05

17 _____

quickly searching for <u>a particular piece or pieces of information</u> in a text
The reader has a question in mind and does not read every word, only key words that will answer the question.

18 _____ _____

the concept that information is <u>stored in long-term memory</u> in <u>networks</u> of connected facts, concepts, and structures, which learners bring to bear on comprehension and production of language

19 _____

background information that a language user brings to bear on a text

20 _____ _____ / _____

grouping ideas into meaningful/semantic clusters to help readers provide some order to a long string of ideas or events from a text

The idea of use this tool is <u>to organize the main ideas of the topic</u> what they are reading. This can be done individually, but it is useful as a productive group work technique as students collectively <u>induce order and hierarchy to a passage</u>.

21 _____

It is a high-speed reading technique that can save the reader time and help him/her get through a text quickly. The reader gets <u>the general sense of a passage (gist)</u>, not specific details.

22 _____

a pedagogical set of procedures for approaching a reading text involving (in sequential order): *survey, question, read, recite, review* strategic investment a certain degree of investment of one's time and effort into using effective strategies for accomplishing L2 goals.

① Survey: skim the text for an overview of main ideas (also through titles, pictures, etc)

② Question: the reader asks questions about what he or she wishes to get out of the text.

③ Read: read the text while looking for answers to the previously formulated questions.

④ Recite: reprocess the salient points of the text through oral and written language.

⑤ Review: assess the importance of what one has just read and incorporate it into long-term associations

23 _____ _____ _____ **(for choosing reading texts)**

Among the three main criteria when choosing texts, it can be considered to be the most important, in that the reading material should <u>interest the students</u> as well as <u>be relevant to their needs</u>. The texts should motivate as well as.
material that students will find interesting, enjoyable, challenging, and appropriate for their goals in learning English

24 _____ _____

By using this processing, readers bring meaning to text based on <u>their experiential background</u> and interpret text based on <u>their prior knowledge</u>. (related to reading skills)
conceptually driven processing in which we draw on our own intelligence and experience to understand a text

Answers

01 Authentic language	**13** Linguistic
02 Basal readers	**14** Literature-based
03 Bottom-up (data-driven) processing	**15** Phonics
04 Content schemata	**16** Readability
05 Exploitability	**17** Scanning
06 Extensive reading	**18** Schema theory
07 Formal schemata	**19** Schemata
08 Guessing	**20** Semantic mapping / Clustering
09 Inferencing	**21** Skimming
10 Intensive reading	**22** SQ3R
11 Interactive processing	**23** Suitability of content
12 Language experience	**24** Top-down (concept-driven) processing

Speaking &
Pronunciation

※ **Review the following Key Terms list and put a checkmark next to Terms that you do not know the exact meaning.**

☐　　Accuracy

☐　　Adjacency pair

☐　　Attention getting

☐　　Conversational gambits

☐　　Chunk / Chunking

☐　　Discourse

☐　　Discourse competence

☐　　Discourse Completion Task (DCT)

☐　　Fluency

☐　　Grammatical competence

☐　　Haptics

☐　　Illocutionary competence

☐　　Illocutionary force

☐　　Information exchange

☐　　Information gap activity

☐　　Intelligibility

☐　　Jigsaw

☐　　Meaningful minimal pairs

☐　　Metalinguistic explanation

☐　　Minimal pairs

☐　　Negotiation of meaning　① comprehension check　② clarification request ③ confirmation check

☐　　Oral dialogue journals

☐　　Perlocutionary force

☐　　Picture description task

☐ Pragmatic competence

☐ Register

☐ Rehearsal

☐ Role-play

☐ Role

☐ Segmentals

☐ Shifting

☐ Simulation

☐ Sociolinguistic competence

06

☐ Speech styles

☐ Storytelling

☐ Strategic competence

☐ Styles

☐ Suprasegmentals

☐ Task type (Richard, 2001) ① jigsaw ② information-gap ③ problem-solving
④ decision-making ⑤ opinion exchange

☐ Termination

☐ Topic clarification

☐ Topic development

☐ Topic nomination

☐ Turn-taking

01 Accuracy (in terms of speaking skills)***

It means that the speakers are required to use the correct vocabulary, grammar, and pronunciation.

02 Adjacency pair (in conversation analysis)***

a sequence of two functionally related turns each made by a different speaker
The second utterance is always a response to the first. Pairs can take various forms, for example:

* invitation - acceptance (or rejection)
* request - acceptance (or denial)
* greeting - greeting
* assessment - agreement (or disagreement)
* blame - denial (or admission)
* question - answer

The response in the second part of the turn can be categorized as preferred or dispreferred. Generally, the preferred second is the shorter, less complicated response, while the dispreferred second tends to be longer and requires more conversational work.

> **Ex 1**
> A: Why don't you come up and see me some time?
> B: I would like to. (preferred)

> **Ex 2**
> A: Uh, if you'd care to come and visit a little while this morning, I'll give you a cup of coffee.
> B: Hehh, well, that's awfully sweet of you. I don't think I can make it this morning, hh umhm, I'm running an ad in the paper uh I have to stay near the phone. (dispreferred)
> (see also **Turn-taking**)

03   Attention getting***

securing the attention of one's audience in a conversation

04   Chunk / Chunking (clustering)***

the act of combining words together as a phrase to seamlessly connect them
Chunking helps your spoken language flow smoothly without having a staggered
or choppy rhythm. Or, in teaching listening, you need to help students to pick out
manageable clusters of words.

06

05   Conversational gambits***

The main way we make our conversation sound natural is by using 'gambits'. A gambit
is a word or phrase which helps us to express what we are trying to say. Gambits
facilitate the flow of conversations.

> **Ex**
>
> *** opening gambits**
> : to start a conversation or to introduce new ideas during a conversation
> · Could I ask..?
> · I'd like to know...
> · Excuse me for interrupting, but...
> · Can I ask a question?
> · First of all,
> · Then,
> · After that,

06 Discourse***

a language (either spoken or written) <u>beyond the sentence level</u>; relationships and rules that govern the connection and interrelationship of sentences within communicative contexts

07 Discourse competence (one of communicative competence)***

the ability to combine ideas to <u>achieve cohesion in form</u> and <u>coherence in thought</u>, above the level of the single sentence

08 Discourse Completion Task (DCT) ⓔ

a data collection instrument that is often used on <u>research on pragmatics</u>
Learners are provided with a <u>scenario</u> in which they must use language to <u>perform some type</u> of action, such as making a request or declining an invitation. Sometimes learners are also provided with an initial utterance to get them started. Then learners are asked to <u>write (or less often, speak) what they would say</u> in the specific context to accomplish the purpose stated in the task.

> **Ex 1**
> You need to borrow a pen from your classmate. What would you say?
>
> **Ex 2**
> You need to ask your teacher for an extension on your homework assignment. What would you say?

09 Formality***

see **speech styles**

10 Fluency***

(a) the unfettered flow of language production or comprehension usually without focal attention on language forms

(b) (in terms of speaking skills) means that the speakers are required to be able to keep going when speaking spontaneously

11 Grammatical competence (or linguistic competence, one of communicative competence)***

the degree to which the language user has mastered the linguistic code, including *vocabulary, grammar, pronunciation, spelling and word formation*

12 Haptics***

any form of nonverbal communication involving touch, also known as kinesthetics

13 Illocutionary competence***

the ability to send and receive intended meanings (see also **language competence**)

14 Illocutionary force***

the intended meaning of the utterance or text within its context (see also **speech acts**)

15 Information exchange***

Task involving two-way communication as in information-gap exercises, when one or both parties (or a larger group) must share information to achieve some goal. Distinguished from Question-answer, or referential activities (which have right or wrong answers) in that sharing of information is critical for the task.

> **Cf**
>
> information gap과 같은 의미로 사용하는 경우도 있다.

> **Ex**
>
> Divide the class in half. For one half of the class (Group A), ask each student to write his/her favorite (1) sport, (2) singer, and (3) actor on a piece of paper. The papers are collected and redistributed to the other half of the class (Group B) at random. Then, ask Group B to mingle with Group A in order to find the person whose favorites they have been given. They are told to ask questions about all three items on the piece of paper. ("Do you like baseball?" or "What's your name?") When everyone has found their partner, they introduce that student to the rest of the class, giving their name and their three favorites.

16 Information gap activity***

In this activity, students are supposed to be working in pairs. One student will have the information that other partner does not have and the partners will share their information. This activity serves many purposes such as *solving a problem* or *collecting information*.

17 Intelligibility***

how clearly a person speaks so that his/her speech is comprehensible to a listener

18   Jigsaw***

a task that requires learners to communicate with each other in order to fill in missing information and to integrate it with other information

19   Meaningful minimal pairs***

contextualized minimal pairs

> **Ex**
> T: The sun is hot on my head!
> S: Then get a *cap*.
> T: Oh, no, I missed the bus. I'm going to be late!
> S: Then get a *cab*.

20   Metalinguistic explanation***

in the classroom, linguistic explanations of rules or patterns in a language
Related to explicit and discrete-point explanations of rules, contrasting with **noticing** or **grammar consciousness raising**
This explains the one side of a continuum for FFI.

21   Minimal pairs***

word pairs that differ by only one sound. For example, "car, tar", "light, white", and "sip, ship" are all examples of minimal pairs. Minimal pairs are important because this single sound difference changes the meaning of the word.

22 Negotiation of meaning***

Negotiation of meaning is a process that speakers go through to reach a clear understanding of each other. Asking for clarification, rephrasing, and confirming what you think you have understood are all strategies for the negotiation of meaning.

① **comprehension check:** A discourse move that involves a speaker in confirming that an interlocutor has understood the meaning of his or her previous utterance. Comprehension checks may result in the provision of modified input if the interlocutor has not understood the previous meaning.

② **clarification request:** An utterance that tries to elicit from a speaker a revised production that is either linguistically more accurate or semantically more transparent. Clarification requests are a common type of corrective feedback because they indicate that there is a problem with the preceding utterance. Clarification requests are argued to be beneficial for learning because they require learners to produce the correct forms themselves, in contrast to other types of feedback that provide the correct form for the learner.

③ **confirmation check:** A confirmation check is discourse move that involves a speaker verifying the meaning of a previous utterance. Confirmation checks are an important component of negotiation of meaning, and are an example of a communication strategy.

23 Oral dialogue journals***

Students create audio recordings of thoughts, reactions, questions, and concerns that the teacher can listen and respond to.

24 Perlocutionary force***

the effect and importance of the consequences of communicative speech acts

25 Picture description task***

a communicative activity that can be used to elicit L2 production
Learners are given a series of pictures that they must describe. Sometimes (a) the pictures are unrelated to each other and are to be described individually. Other times, (b) learners must use the pictures to create a narrative, based either on the order of pictures provided for them or by putting the pictures into a logical order themselves. Learners can perform these tasks either by themselves or with other learners in an information gap task.

26 Pragmatic competence***

the ability to produce and comprehend functional and sociolinguistic aspects of language; *illocutionary competence*

27 Register***

the style of language that is appropriate in a given context
The different types of language that are used in more or less formal contexts are examples of different registers.

> **Ex 1**
> Ain't got no lovin' vs I don't have any significant other in my life

In addition, register may refer to specialist language that is used in different professions or hobbies.

> **Ex 2**
> morpheme, interlanguage, and focus on form are part of the register of SLA

28　Rehearsal***

(a) an aspect of some definitions of noticing in which linguistic input is repeated in short-term memory. Such rehearsal is said to be an important component of turning intake into learned knowledge.
(b) the act of <u>practicing or repeating an utterance or task</u> before producing it. Rehearsal can take place internally in the learner's mind or it can be done verbally.

29　Role-play(s)***

(a) giving a role to one or more members of a group and assigning an objective or purpose that participants must accomplish
(b) Students pretend they are in various social contexts and have a variety of social roles. In this activity, the teacher gives information to the learners such as who they are and what they think or feel.

30　Role(s)***

functions or positions that a teacher or students have in a particular activity or in the classroom

31　Segmentals (teaching pronunciation)***

Bottom-up approach
It begins with <u>the articulation of individual sounds</u> and works up towards intonation, stress and rhythm. In the bottom-up approach, the basic idea is that if you teach the segments, the suprasegmental features will take care of by themselves.

32 Shifting (of a topic)***

changing the subject in a conversation

33 Simulation(s)***

These are very similar to role-plays but this is more elaborate. Students can bring items to the class to create a realistic environment. For instance, if a student is acting as a singer, she brings a microphone to sing and so on.

34 Sociolinguistic competence (one of communicative competence)***

the extent to which utterances can be used or understood appropriately in various social contexts
It includes knowledge of *speech acts* and functions such as *persuading, apologizing and describing.*

35 Speech styles***

five speech styles, depending on their degree of formality
① Frozen style (or Fixed speech): A speech style is characterized by the use of certain grammar and vocabulary particular to a certain field, one in which the speaker is inserted. The language in this speech style is very formal and static, making it one of the highest forms of speech styles. It's usually done in a format where the speaker talks and the audience listens without actually being given the space to respond.

② Formal style: This style, just like the previous one, is also characterized by a formal (agreed upon and even documented) vocabulary and choice of words, yet it's more universal as it doesn't necessarily require expertise in any field and it's not as rigid as the frozen style.

The language in this speech is respectful and rejects the use of slang, contractions, ellipses and qualifying modal adverbials. Oftentimes the speaker must plan the sentences before delivering them.

③ Consultative style: The third level of communication it's a style characterized by a semi-formal vocabulary, often unplanned and reliant on the listener's responses and overall participation.

④ Casual style (or Informal style): As the name says, this style is characterized by its casualty, with a flexible and informal vocabulary that may include slang. It's usually unplanned, pretty relaxed, and reliant on the fluid back and forth between those involved, without any particular order.

⑤ Intimate style: This is the speech style that's reserved for people who have a really close connection. It's casual and relaxed and goes beyond words, as it incorporates nonverbal communication and even personal language codes, such as terms of endearment and expressions whose meaning are only understood by the participants, besides slang.

36 Storytelling***

Students can briefly summarize a tale or story they heard from somebody beforehand, or they may create their own stories to tell their classmates. It fosters creative thinking.

37 Strategic competence (one of communicative competence)***

the ability to use strategies like gestures or "talking around" an unknown word in order to overcome limitations in language knowledge; the use of appropriate body (non-verbal) language

38   Styles (in speech discourse)^{***}

conventions for selecting words, phrases, discourse, and nonverbal language in specified contexts, such as *intimate, casual, and consultative styles*

39   Suprasegmentals (teaching pronunciation)^{***}

Top-down approach
It begins with patterns of intonation, stress and rhythm and brings separate sounds into sharper focus as and when required. The assumption is that once the prosodic features are in place, the necessary segmental discriminations will follow accordingly.

40   Task type (Richard, 2001)^{***}

① Jigsaw: a communicative activity in which two or more interlocutors have differing pieces of information that must be combined in order to complete successfully the activity. For example, learners may be given different components of a character's daily activities, with the goal of the task being for the learners to recreate the character's routine. Learners must share their information in order to complete the entire routine. The jigsaw task is identified following characteristics:

   ⓐ Each interactant holds a different portion of information which must be exchanged and manipulated in order to reach the task outcome.

   ⓑ Both interactants are required to request and supply this information to each other.

   ⓒ Interactants have the same or convergent goals.

   ⓓ Only one acceptable outcome is possible from their attempts to meet this goal.

As jigsaw task interactants, X and Y hold dual roles as information holders, suppliers, and requesters, each having a piece of the 'puzzle' which must be joined together. The task participants are expected to achieve a convergent goal and a single outcome which allow no options, in order to complete the task. Thus, Pica claims that "this task can be considered the type of task most likely to generate opportunities for interactants to work toward comprehension, feedback, and interlangauge modification processes related to successful SLA".

② Information-gap: pedagogical tasks in which different learners each have part of the information required to complete the task, usually to solve a problem or make a decision. (Simply put, task requires that one person describes a picture and the other person draws the picture.) For example, learners may be asked to find a lost friend and each be given different information about him, such as the country where he is or the type of work he does. To find the person, the learners have to exchange the information that they have. An information gap task is defined as <u>one participant holding information that the other does not already know</u>, but needs to know in order to complete a task. The gap in the distribution of information results in a one-way flow of information from the sending one interactant (X) to the receiving interactant (Y). Thus, interactants have less of a chance to modify production toward greater comprehensibility since the task assigns each interactant a fixed role. Although the "information gap" task limits interlanguage modification, the activity has been even more widely used than the jigsaw in language teaching and learning, particularly in characterizing activities which motivate communication among classroom language learners.

③ Problem-solving: A problem-solving task is characterized as a task oriented toward a <u>single resolution</u> of outcome. In this task, information is expected to flow two ways, but participation of all students is not necessary for successful completion of the exercise.

④ Decision-making: A decision-making task has a number of possible outcomes available to participants in contrast to the problem-solving task. The decision-making participants can choose to seek, withhold, or exchange information and reach one of many possible decisions as they work to complete this task. Such discussion tasks are open-ended and do not require the participation of all students. There is also no expectation of convergence of opinions to any particular outcome.

⑤ Opinion exchange: The opinion exchange task, which engages learners <u>in discussion and exchange of ideas</u> is also not expected to converge toward a single goal, but any number of outcome options, including no outcome at all, is possible for participants. To complete the task, interaction is possible but not required by the participant and even a single interactant might dominate. Moral, ethical, religious, and political issues are often sensitive, "hot" topics for classroom debates, arguments, and discussions. Students can get involved in the content-centered nature of such activity and thus pave the way for automatic processing of language itself. Here are a few such issues: woman's right, privacy rights and government "snooping", euthanasia, environmental crises, etc.

41 Termination (of a topic)***

in a conversation, the process of ending the conversation

42 Topic clarification***

in a conversation, asking questions to remove perceived ambiguities in another's utterance

43 Topic development***

maintaining a topic in a conversation

44 Topic nomination***

proposing a topic for discussion in a conversation

45 Turn-taking***

in a conversation, conventions in which participants allow appropriate opportunities for others to talk, or "take the floor"

※ **Read the following descriptions and fill in the blanks.**

01 _____

a language (either spoken or written) beyond the sentence level; relationships and rules that govern the connection and interrelationship of sentences within communicative contexts

02 _____ _____ **(one of communicative competence)**

the ability to combine ideas to achieve cohesion in form and coherence in thought, above the level of the single sentence

03 _____

(a) the unfettered flow of language production or comprehension usually without focal attention on language forms
(b) (in terms of speaking skills) means that the speakers are required to be able to keep going when speaking spontaneously

04 _____ _____ **(or linguistic competence, one of communicative competence)**

the degree to which the language user has mastered the linguistic code, including *vocabulary, grammar, pronunciation, spelling and word formation*

05 _____ _____

the ability to send and receive intended meanings (see also **language competence**)

06 _____ _____ _____

In this activity, students are supposed to be <u>working in pairs</u>. One student will have the information that other partner does not have and the partners will <u>share their information</u>. This activity serves many purposes such as *solving a problem or collecting information.*

07 _____

how clearly a person speaks so that <u>his/her speech is comprehensible</u> to a listener

08 _____

a task that <u>requires learners to communicate</u> with each other in order to <u>fill in missing</u> information and to <u>integrate it</u> with other information

09 _____ _____

the effect and importance of <u>the consequences</u> of communicative speech acts

10 _____ _____ _____

a communicative activity that can be used to elicit L2 production
Learners are given <u>a series of pictures</u> that they must describe. Sometimes (a) the pictures are unrelated to each other and are to <u>be described individually</u>. Other times, (b) learners must use the pictures to <u>create a narrative</u>, based either on the order of pictures provided for them or by putting the pictures <u>into a logical order themselves</u>. Learners can perform these tasks either by themselves or with other learners in an information gap task.

11 _____ _____

the ability to produce and comprehend functional and sociolinguistic aspects of language; *illocutionary competence*

12 _____

the style of language that is appropriate in a given context
The different types of language that are used in more or less formal contexts are examples of different THESE.

> **Ex 1**
> Ain't got no lovin' vs I don't have any significant other in my life

In addition, THIS may refer to specialist language that is used in different professions or hobbies.

> **Ex 2**
> morpheme, interlanguage, and focus on form are part of the register of SLA

13 _____

(a) an aspect of some definitions of noticing in which linguistic input is repeated in short-term memory. THIS is said to be an important component of turning intake into learned knowledge.
(b) the act of practicing or repeating an utterance or task before producing it. THIS can take place internally in the learner's mind or it can be done verbally.

14 _____

(a) giving a role to one or more members of a group and assigning an objective or purpose that participants must accomplish
(b) Students pretend they are in various social contexts and have a variety of social roles. In this activity, the teacher gives information to the learners such as who they are and what they think or feel.

15 _____

functions or positions that a teacher or students have in a particular activity or in the classroom

16 _____ **(teaching pronunciation)**

Bottom-up approach
It begins with the articulation of individual sounds and works up towards intonation, stress and rhythm. In the bottom-up approach, the basic idea is that if you teach the segments, the suprasegmental features will take care of by themselves.

17 _____

These are very similar to role-plays but this is more elaborate. Students can bring items to the class to create a realistic environment. For instance, if a student is acting as a singer, she brings a microphone to sing and so on.

18 _____ _____ **(one of communicative competence)**

the extent to which utterances can be used or understood appropriately in various social contexts
It includes knowledge of *speech acts* and functions such as *persuading, apologizing and describing.*

19 _____

Students can briefly summarize a tale or story they heard from somebody beforehand, or they may create their own stories to tell their classmates. It fosters creative thinking.

20 _____ _____ **(one of communicative competence)**

the ability to <u>use strategies</u> like gestures or "talking around" an unknown word in order to <u>overcome limitations in language knowledge</u>; <u>the use of appropriate body(non-verbal) language</u>

21 _____ **(in speech discourse)**

<u>conventions</u> for selecting words, phrases, discourse, and nonverbal language <u>in specified contexts</u>, such as *intimate, casual, and consultative* _____

22 _____ **(teaching pronunciation)**

Top-down approach
It begins with <u>patterns of intonation, stress and rhythm</u> and brings separate sounds into sharper focus as and when required. The assumption is that once the prosodic features are in place, the necessary segmental discriminations will follow accordingly.

23 _____ **(of a topic)**

in a conversation, the process of ending the conversation

24 _____ _____

in a conversation, asking questions to remove perceived ambiguities in another's utterance

25 _____ _____

maintaining a topic in a conversation

26 _____ _____

proposing a topic for discussion in a conversation

27 _____

in a conversation, conventions in which participants allow appropriate opportunities for others to talk, or "take the floor"

Answers

01 Discourse

02 Discourse competence

03 Fluency

04 Grammatical competence

05 Illocutionary competence

06 Information gap activity

07 Intelligibility

08 Jigsaw

09 Perlocutionary force

10 Picture description task

11 Pragmatic competence

12 Register

13 Rehearsal

14 Role-play(s)

15 Role(s)

16 Segmentals

17 Simulation(s)

18 Sociolinguistic competence

19 Storytelling

20 Strategic competence

21 Styles

22 Suprasegmentals

23 Termination

24 Topic clarification

25 Topic development

26 Topic nomination

27 Turn-taking

Note

Writing

※ **Review the following Key Terms list and put a checkmark next to Terms that you do not know the exact meaning.**

- ☐ Brainstorming
- ☐ Checklist
- ☐ Composing
- ☐ Conference(ing)
- ☐ Contrastive rhetoric
- ☐ Controlled writing
- ☐ Dialogue journal(s)
- ☐ Dictocomp / Dicto-composition
- ☐ Discourse
- ☐ Display writing
- ☐ Error Correction Code (ECC)
- ☐ Formality
- ☐ Freewriting
- ☐ Genre
- ☐ Genre-based approach/writing
- ☐ Guided writing
- ☐ Intercultural rhetoric
- ☐ Peer-editing
- ☐ Process-oriented approach
- ☐ Product-oriented approach
- ☐ Self-writing
- ☐ Real writing
- ☐ Rhetorical formality (in writing)
- ☐ Sentence combining

01 Brainstorming***

open-ended, rapid-fire voluntary oral or written listing of ideas with no debate or evaluation by others

02 Checklist***

The teacher can make a checklist which asks editors to check for the various areas in a piece of writing. It may ask editors, "Does the introduction contain a hook?", "Does the paper have a well-defined thesis?", "Do all the paragraphs have strong supporting sentences?", and so forth. It's best that teachers model an example of how to use this with an example well-written passage and a poorly-written one and respond to them with a copy of this for each on an overhead projector for comparison.

03 Composing [Ⓔ]

the thinking, drafting, and revising procedures involved in planned writing

04 Conference(ing)***

Teachers should meet with individual students to comment and give advice on assignments. This provides a student with a chance to discuss the strengths and weaknesses of his writing with the teacher. Teachers should remind students that academic progress rests on the student's shoulders and not the teacher's.

05 Contrastive rhetoric [Ⓔ]

L1 schemata and patterns of thinking and writing can carry over into L2 writing. (see **intercultural rhetoric**)

06 Controlled writing***

Teachers typically present a short text to students in which they <u>must alter a given structure</u> throughout. (**Ex** convert all present tense verbs to past tense)

07 Dialogue journal(s)***

A dialogue journal is where <u>a student writes down their thoughts, feeling, and reactions.</u> Although it's meant for the student, both the student and the instructor are its readers, as the instructor reads and responds to the entries.

These are <u>written conversations</u> in which a learner and teacher (or another writing partner) <u>communicate regularly</u> (daily, weekly, or on a schedule that fits the educational setting) over a semester, school year, or course. Learners write as much as they choose on a wide range of topics and in a variety of genres and styles. The teacher writes back regularly, responding to questions and comments, introducing new topics, or asking questions.

08 Dictocomp / Dicto-composition***

A paragraph is read at normal speed, usually two or three times; then the teacher asks students to <u>re-write the paragraph to the best of their recollection</u> of the reading. In one of several variations of this technique, the teacher, after reading the passage, puts key words from the paragraph, in sequence, on the chalkboard as cues for the students.

09   Discourse***

a language (either spoken or written) <u>beyond the sentence level</u>; relationships and rules that govern the connection and interrelationship of sentences within communicative contexts

10   Display writing***

primarily for the display of a student's knowledge, as opposed to *real writing*

11   Error Correction Code (ECC)***

This is a common tool to optimize <u>learning opportunities from mistakes</u> learners make in written work and to encourage the editing stages of process writing. Teachers show the learners <u>where</u> the mistakes are and <u>what kind</u> they are, and then learners try to correct the errors as a second stage to the initial writing task.

> **Ex**
> SP: Spelling error, P: Punctuation/capitalization, VT: Verb tense, WC: Word choice,
> WF: Word form

12   Formality***

It refers to <u>prescribed forms that certain written messages must adhere to</u>. We have rhetorical, or organizational, formality in essay writing that demands <u>a writer's conformity to conventions</u> like paragraph topics. There is usually a logical order for, say, comparing and contrasting something; opening and closing essay, and a preference for nonredundancy and subordination of clauses, and more.

13 Freewriting***

writing simply to start the "flow" of writing, with little thought to grammaticality, spelling, logical thinking, or organization

14 Genre***

a category of discourse characterized by similarities in form, style, or subject matter (Ex academic essay, poem, business letter)

15 Genre-based approach / writing***

The genre approach to teaching writing is mainly concerned, as the name indicates, on teaching particular genres that students need control of in order to succeed in particular situations. This might include an emphasis on the content of the text as well as the context in which the text is produced. The fundamental principle that underlies the genre approach is that language is functional; that is, it is through language that we achieve certain goals. Three essential features of the genre:

(a) the context, which includes the situation and audience
(b) the content, which indicates the information and message conveyed
(c) the construction, that is, how the texts of the genre are typically constructed in terms of the layout and language

16 Guided writing***

It loosens the teacher's control compared to controlled writing. Teachers provide a series of stimulators (Ex asking students a series of questions), which enables them to tell a story just viewed on a videotape.

17 Intercultural rhetoric***

accounting for the richness of <u>rhetorical variation of written texts</u>, the varying contexts in which they are constructed, and <u>the cultural characteristics</u> of writing (see also **contrastive rhetoric**)

18 Peer-editing***

Editing a peer's piece of writing
Some students may see this as unbeneficial to learning and may prefer teachers to do all the editing. This allows students to <u>identify each other's strengths and weaknesses</u> in their writing skills while being <u>less reliant on the teacher</u>. When students experience this, they become more empowered, and more objective in their writing.

07

19 Process-oriented approach***

Focus on <u>the steps</u> that go into writing. Giving and receiving feedback and creating <u>multiple drafts</u>. Initial focus on ideas/content.

20 Product-oriented approach***

Focus on 'getting it right'. <u>Controlled tasks</u> following models. Final product evaluated.

21 Real writing***

the reader does not know the answer (to a question or problem) and genuinely wants information, as opposed to *display writing*.
<u>Peer-editing</u> provides real writing opportunity, as do various forms of informal <u>writing</u> like diaries, letters, postcards, notes, and personal messages.

22 Rhetorical formality (in writing)***

organizational conventions in writing for connecting sentences, showing relationships, opening paragraphs, using subordination, and so on, that extend beyond the sentence level

23 Self-writing***

writing with only the self in mind as an audience
The most salient instance of this category in classrooms is note-taking where students take notes during a lecture for the purpose of later recall. Diary or journal writing also falls into this category.

24 Sentence combining***

This activity encourages a writer to take two or more short, choppy sentences and combine them into one effective sentence. By learning this skill, students enhance their writing style. Such skill is something that will develop over several short practice sessions and should be considered as one component of an overall writing program.

※ **Read the following descriptions and fill in the blanks.**

01 _____

open-ended, rapid-fire voluntary oral or written listing of ideas with no debate or evaluation by others

02 _____

The teacher can make THIS which asks editors to check for the various areas in a piece of writing. It may ask editors, "Does the introduction contain a hook?", "Does the paper have a well-defined thesis?", "Do all the paragraphs have strong supporting sentences?", and so forth. It's best that teachers model an example of how to use this with an example well-written passage and a poorly-written one and respond to them with a copy of this for each on an overhead projector for comparison.

03 _____

Teachers should meet with individual students to comment and give advice on assignments. This provides a student with a chance to discuss the strengths and weaknesses of his writing with the teacher. Teachers should remind students that academic progress rests on the student's shoulders and not the teacher's.

04 _____   _____

Teachers typically present a short text to students in which they must alter a given structure throughout. (Ex convert all present tense verbs to past tense)

05

_____   _____

It is where a student writes down their thoughts, feeling, and reactions. Although it's meant for the student, both the student and the instructor are its readers, as the instructor reads and responds to the entries.

These are written conversations in which a learner and teacher (or another writing partner) communicate regularly (daily, weekly, or on a schedule that fits the educational setting) over a semester, school year, or course. Learners write as much as they choose on a wide range of topics and in a variety of genres and styles. The teacher writes back regularly, responding to questions and comments, introducing new topics, or asking questions.

06

_____ / _____

A paragraph is read at normal speed, usually two or three times; then the teacher asks students to re-write the paragraph to the best of their recollection of the reading. In one of several variations of this technique, the teacher, after reading the passage, puts key words from the paragraph, in sequence, on the chalkboard as cues for the students.

07

_____

a language (either spoken or written) beyond the sentence level; relationships and rules that govern the connection and interrelationship of sentences within communicative contexts

08

_____   _____

primarily for the display of a student's knowledge, as opposed to *real writing*

09 _____ _____ _____

This is a common tool to optimize <u>learning opportunities from mistakes</u> learners make in written work and to encourage the editing stages of process writing. Teachers show the learners <u>where</u> the mistakes are and <u>what kind</u> they are, and then learners try to correct the errors as a second stage to the initial writing task.

>
> SP: Spelling error, P: Punctuation/capitalization, VT: Verb tense, WC: Word choice, WF: Word form

07

10 _____

writing simply to <u>start the "flow" of writing</u>, with little thought to grammaticality, spelling, logical thinking, or organization

11 _____ **approach / writing**

The genre approach to teaching writing is mainly concerned, as the name indicates, on teaching <u>particular genres</u> that students need control of in order to succeed <u>in particular situations</u>. This might include an emphasis on the content of the text as well as the context in which the text is produced. The fundamental principle that underlies the genre approach is that <u>language is functional</u>; that is, it is through language that we achieve certain goals. Three essential features of the genre:

(a) the context, which includes the situation and audience
(b) the content, which indicates the information and message conveyed
(c) the construction, that is, how the texts of the genre are typically constructed in terms of the layout and language

12 _____ _____

It loosens the teacher's control compared to controlled writing. Teachers provide a series of stimulators (**Ex** asking students a series of questions), which enables them to tell a story just viewed on a videotape.

13 _____ _____

accounting for the richness of <u>rhetorical variation of written texts</u>, the varying contexts in which they are constructed, and <u>the cultural characteristics of writing</u> (see also **contrastive rhetoric**)

14 _____

Editing a peer's piece of writing
Some students may see this as unbeneficial to learning and may prefer teachers to do all the editing. This allows students to <u>identify each other's strengths and weaknesses</u> in their writing skills while being <u>less reliant on the teacher</u>. When students experience this, they become more empowered, and more objective in their writing.

15 _____ **approach**

Focus on <u>the steps</u> that go into writing. Giving and receiving feedback and creating <u>multiple drafts</u>. Initial focus on ideas/content.

16 _____ **approach**

Focus on 'getting it right'. <u>Controlled tasks</u> following models. Final product evaluated.

17 _____ _____

the reader does not know the answer (to a question or problem) and genuinely wants information, as opposed to *display writing*.

<u>Peer-editing</u> provides real writing opportunity, as do various forms of informal <u>writing like diaries, letters, postcards, notes, and personal messages.</u>

18 _____ _____ **(in writing)**

<u>organizational conventions</u> in writing for connecting sentences, showing relationships, opening paragraphs, using subordination, and so on, that extend <u>beyond the sentence level</u>

19 _____ _____

This activity encourages a writer to take two or more <u>short, choppy sentences and combine them</u> into one effective sentence. By learning this skill, students enhance <u>their writing style.</u> Such skill is something that will develop over several short practice sessions and should be considered as one component of an overall writing program.

Answers

01 Brainstorming

02 Checklist

03 Conference(ing)

04 Controlled writing

05 Dialogue journal(s)

06 Dictocomp / Dicto-composition

07 Discourse

08 Display writing

09 Error correction code

10 Freewriting

11 Genre-based

12 Guided writing

13 Intercultural rhetoric

14 Peer-editing

15 Process-oriented

16 Product-oriented

17 Real writing

18 Rhetorical formality

19 Sentence combining

Vocabulary & Grammar

※ **Review the following Key Terms list and put a checkmark next to Terms that you do not know the exact meaning.**

☐　Abductive approach

☐　Accuracy

☐　Appropriateness

☐　Attention

☐　Awareness

☐　Awareness-raising

☐　Breadth of knowledge

☐　Collocation

☐　Complexity

☐　Concordance

☐　Concordancer

☐　Concordancing

☐　Connotation

☐　Consciousness-raising task

☐　Corpora

☐　Corpus linguistics

☐　Declarative knowledge

☐　Deductive approach

☐　Deductive reasoning

☐　Depth of knowledge

☐　Dictogloss

☐　Dimensions of grammar

☐　Drill(s)

☐　Explicit instruction

☐　Explicit knowledge

- ☐ Explicit (treatment of form)
- ☐ Focus on Form (FonF)
- ☐ Focus on Forms (FonFs)
- ☐ Focus on meaning
- ☐ Form (of language)
- ☐ Form-focused Instruction (FFI)
- ☐ Frequency
- ☐ Garden path
- ☐ Global error(s)
- ☐ Grammaring
- ☐ Grammaticality
- ☐ Grammaticalization
- ☐ Hypercorrection
- ☐ Implicit instruction
- ☐ Implicit knowledge
- ☐ Implicit learning
- ☐ Implicit (treatment of form)
- ☐ Incidental learning
- ☐ Inductive approach
- ☐ Inductive reasoning
- ☐ Input enhancement
- ☐ Input flooding
- ☐ Input processing
- ☐ Intentional learning
- ☐ Keyword method / technique
- ☐ Lexical approach
- ☐ Lexicogrammatical approach
- ☐ Local error(s)
- ☐ Meaningful drills

08

- ☐ Mechanical drills
- ☐ PPP
- ☐ Procedural knowledge
- ☐ Processing instruction
- ☐ Productive knowledge
- ☐ Receptive knowledge
- ☐ Restructuring
- ☐ Salience
- ☐ Structured input
- ☐ Structured input activities
- ☐ Structured output
- ☐ Teachability hypothesis
- ☐ Vocabulary analysis (=word analysis)
- ☐ Word family(ies)
- ☐ Word formation
- ☐ Word map
- ☐ Word-learning strategies

01   Abductive approach***

It involves the learners understanding <u>hidden rules</u> of language use through the process of <u>exploring hypotheses and inferences</u>.

Abduction refers to the exploratory process of trying out tentative solutions to problems or facts to figure out what may happen, to see if they work, or to experience something new. (Cunningham, 2002) Language teachers can start with abduction, taking experiential and exploratory approaches (puzzle-based learning) and then move on to either inductive or deductive tasks as relevant, followed with further exploration at a wider or deeper level.

Ex

* Abduction in the L2 classroom

1. Select an authentic text that includes specific linguistic features you want to emphasize (for example, input enhancement for relative clauses).
2. Create an activity that targets these linguistic features (for example, a map activity with an information gap that incorporates relative clauses).
3. Have students work in groups to identify and note the grammatical features or patterns present in the text.
4. Ask students to present their observations to the entire class.

Expansion:

5. Inductive approach: After identifying patterns, students gather additional examples that illustrate these patterns and develop a general rule based on their findings.
6. Deductive approach: Together, the teacher and students develop a grammatical rule, verify it using a grammar book, and examine further examples that demonstrate this rule.

---

02   Accuracy***

The correct use of target language, 'correct' generally interpreted as meaning 'according to L1 speaker usage'. Accuracy is most often used to refer to grammar, but the term may also apply to pronunciation, vocabulary, and pragmatics. Accuracy is often <u>measured together with fluency and complexity</u> in order to provide <u>an overall view</u> of learners' L2 production capabilites.

03 Appropriateness***

Using appropriate language means that a speaker's language is suitable or fitting for themselves, as the speaker; our audience; the speaking context; and the speech itself. Students need to know if a particular lexical item is usually used in writing or in speech; or in formal or informal discourse.

04 Attention***

the psychological process of focusing on certain stimuli to the exclusion of others

05 Awareness [Ⓔ]

conscious attention, cognizance of linguistic, mental, or emotional factors through attention and focus

06 Awareness-raising [Ⓔ]

calling a learner's attention to linguistic factors that may not otherwise be noticed

07 Breadth of knowledge***

This term is used primarily in vocabulary acquisition to refer to the size of a learner's vocabulary. It is concerned with the number of words that a learner knows, either productively or receptively. As such, the term contrasts with depth of knowledge, which refers to how much learners know about specific words. Some researchers argue that knowledge of the 3,000 most common words in a language will enable a learner to study in that language with relative ease.

08   Collocation***

A collocation is a group of words that often occur together. For example, in English one 'plays tennis' but 'goes skiing'. There are often no fixed rules for collocations and they are often one of the last components of vocabulary that L2 learners learn.

09   Complexity***

(a) Complexity refers to language production that expresses multiple ideas within a sentence by using subordination. In this sense, it is one way to measure a language learner's ability in the second language in addition to fluency and accuracy.

(b) Complexity is a measure of the degree to which an activity involving language requires greater amounts of mental effort and attention. Complexity can be varied by task designers, for example by asking learners to pay attention to more than one feature in a task.

(c) the lexical variety and syntactic elaborateness of the learner's linguistic system

(d) (related to reading skills) The linguistic differences between speech and writing are one of major contributing cause to difficulty. Writing and speech represent different modes of complexity, and the most salient difference is in the nature of clauses. Spoken language tends to have shorter clauses connected by more coordinate conjunctions, while writing has longer clauses and more subordination. The shorter clauses are often a factor of the **redundancy** we build into speech (repeating subjects and verbs for clarity).

> **Ex**
>
> The cognitive complexity of versions (1) and (2) are not different. But structurally, four sentences were used in version (b) to replace the one lone sentence of version (a).
>
> (1) Because of the frequent ambiguity that therefore is present in a good deal of writing, readers must do their best to infer, to interpret, and to "read between the lines". (Written version)
>
> (2) There's frequent ambiguity in a lot of writing. And so, readers have to infer a lot. They also have to interpret what they read. And sometimes they have to "read between the lines". (Spoken version)

(e) (related to writing skills) Writers must learn the discourse features of written L2, how to create syntactic and lexical variety, how to combine sentences, and more. Sentence combining can pose some difficulty for learners of English. Learning to use coordinating and subordinating clauses effectively in writing poses a challenge even for native English users.

10   Concordance***

It is an alphabetical list of the principal words used in a book or body of work, listing every instance of each word with its immediate context. The sample of concordance can provide students with instances of real language use helping learners to know how to use language that is appropriate in different contexts.

11   Concordancer***

This is a computer program that automatically constructs a concordance.

12   Concordancing***

indexing of words that enables one to reference words in the multiple possible contexts in which they appear in spoken or written language consciousness-raising, drawing students' attention to formal elements of language within the context of meaningful communication and tasks

Concordancing allows learners to see words in context, while the extensive corpora serve as databanks that facilitate a deeper examination and understanding of the relationships between grammatical and lexical units.

13   Connotation***

The connotations of a word are the emotional or positive-negative associations that is implies. A closely related word is implication.

14 Consciousness-raising task (CR task)***

A task that involves inductively drawing learners' attention to characteristics of the target language. As such, they do not aim to enable learners to produce the target form; instead, the goals is for learners to become aware of specific L2 characteristics so that they can notice them in the input. An example of a CR task would be to provide learners with a group of sentences that contain examples of a specific rule. Learners would induce the rule by looking at the sentences and then writing out the rule after they have identified it. Ellis et al. (2001) define CR task as a pedagogic activity where the learners are provided with second language data in some form and required to perform some operation on it, the purpose of which is to arrive at an explicit understanding of the target grammar. CR task seems to be similar to the PPP (presentation, practice, production) model, but one significant difference is clear. In the PPP model, students are required to use a target form in speaking or writing. However, in CR, task what learners should be able to do is not to use the form in speaking and writing but to find the rule and understand the target form in terms of form, meaning, and function.

08

15 Corpora***

plural of corpus

16 Corpus linguistics***

an approach to linguistic research that relies on computer analyses of a collection of text-written, transcribed speech or both stored in electronic form and analyzed with digital software

17 Declarative knowledge***

knowledge about something
Consciously known and verbalizable facts, knowledge, and information. This enables a student to describe a rule of grammar and apply it in pattern practice drills.

18 Deductive approach***

It involves the learners being given a general rule, which is then applied to specific language examples and honed through practice exercises.

19 Deductive reasoning Ⓔ

moving from a generalization to specific instances in which subsumed fact are inferred from a general principle

20 Depth of knowledge***

a term, primarily associated with vocabulary learning, that describes the amount of information that a learner knows about a specific word
Learners may only know the basis form and meaning of a word, or they may have a deeper knowledge of the word, such as its *derivational forms*, its *collocations* or its *connotations*. (Ex knowing the verb *break*, and also *take a break* and *break up*)

21 Dictogloss***

a variation on the dictocomp technique
It is a task-based procedure designed to help L2 learners internalize certain grammatical elements that are built into a text. Through the reconstruction of a text, students come to notice certain grammatical features. Before the reconstruction stage, students are not asked to notice a grammatical form, even though they are embedded in the text. Only at the last stage of the procedure will students possibly become aware of using the form.

22 Dimensions of grammar Ⓑ

form, meaning, and use
* **form:** observable structural components such as phonemes, graphemes, inflectional morphemes, and syntactic patterns

* **meaning:** the semantic level of the structural items including lexical and grammatical meaning

* **use:** meanings of utterances across different contexts and cohesion in discourse

23   Drill(s)***

a <u>mechanical technique</u> focusing on a minimal number of language forms through repetition

Drills offer students an opportunity to listen and to orally repeat certain strings of language that may pose some linguistic difficulty - either phonological or grammatical. They allow students to focus on one element of language in a controlled activity.

<Guidelines for successful drills>
· Keep them simple (just one point at a time).
· Keep them short (a few minutes of a class hour).
· Limit them to phonological, morphological, or syntactic points.
· Make sure they ultimately lead to communicative goals.

08

24   Explicit instruction***

language teaching that draws attention to language items and language rules in a clear manner and <u>with the express purpose of teaching those linguistic items and rules</u>
Explicit instruction involves the overt presentation of rules of the L2. This can be done <u>both deductively and inductively.</u>

25   Explicit knowledge***

information that a person knows about language, and usually, the <u>ability to articulate that information</u>

26　Explicit (treatment of form)^{***}

drawing learners' focal attention to formal elements of language, as opposed to *implicit treatment*

27　Focus on Form (FonF)^{***}

an approach that attempts to induce learners' incidental learning by drawing their attention to target forms while they are engaged in communicative activities (see also **form-focused instruction**)

28　Focus on Forms (FonFs)^{***}

THIS involves more traditional approaches to grammar that consist of isolating individual linguistic constructs out of context. ("the use of some kind of synthetic syllabus and/or a linguistically isolating teaching method, such as audiolingualism, the Silent Way, or Total Physical Response")

29　Focus on meaning^{***}

THIS does not allow for any attention whatsoever to the linguistic code of the L2. The assumption behind this approach is that an L2 is learned best by allowing students to experience the L2 through communication and not through rigorous study. (**Ex**) Krashen's Natural Approach, immersion programs)

30　Form (of language)^{***}

unit of language, such as morphemes, words, grammar rules, discourse rules, and other organizational elements of language

31 Form-focused Instruction (FFI)***

any pedagogical effort used to draw a learner's <u>attention to language form either</u>
<u>implicitly or explicitly</u>
A range of instructional methods that direct learners' attention to language items. As
such, FFI contrasts with meaning-focused instruction. It is generally divided into two
main categories: *focus on forms* (Ex grammar translation and PPP) and *focus on form*
(Ex input flood and input enhancement)

32 Frequency***

<u>the number of times that a linguistic item occurs</u> in either input or output, in a given
amount of time
Various researchers have asserted that learners should receive explicit instruction and
practice for the first two to three thousand *High frequency words* and beyond this
threshold level, most *Low frequency words* will be learned implicitly while reading or
listening. The reason is that it is very difficult to guess the meaning of new words unless
many words on a page are known.

33 Garden path***

This is the most explicit technique. A teacher takes learners into <u>making</u>
<u>overgeneralization</u> regarding a grammatical rule so that the learners can notice the form
more impressively. That is, when a teacher plans to teach a certain target form, the
teacher <u>only briefly explains the major rules</u> of the form instead of its exceptions. Then,
the teacher corrects students' errors, providing the rule of the exceptions when students'
overgeneralization actually occur.

34 Global error(s)***

errors that <u>hinder communication</u> or prevents a hearer (or reader) from comprehending
some aspect of a message

35   Grammaring***

(Larsen-freeman 2003)
It refers to the organic process of using grammar constructions accurately, meaningfully, and appropriately. It shifts the focus from the product of learning static grammar rules to the process of using grammar in real world communicative contexts. The notion of grammaring helps us move away from the usual traditions of teaching grammar as a body of knowledge and instead treats grammar as a skill to develop.

36   Grammaticality ᴱ

conforming to the systematic use of the target language
L1 speakers do not always agree in what they feel is grammatical due to regional variation or feelings related to socially acceptable forms of the language.

37   Grammaticalization ᴱ

It describes the process involved when learners begin to use the L2.

> **Ex**
> No very good. (Not using grammatical structures.)
> → It's not very good. (As developing interlanguage system, learners are able to use grammatical structures. That is, grammaticalization occurs.)

38   Hypercorrection***

a phenomenon in which language speakers overuses language rules in contexts where they do not apply
A speaker or writer who produces a hypercorrection generally believes through a misunderstanding of such rules that the form is more "correct", standard, or otherwise preferable, often combined with a desire to appear formal or educated. For example, the correction of the subject-positioned "you and me" to "you and I" leads people to

"internalize the rule that 'you and I' is somehow more proper, and they end up using it in places where they should not – such as 'he gave it to you and I' when it should be 'he gave it to you and me.'" Often, the linguistic form being overused in seen as being socially more prestigious. (see also **overgenerlization**)

39 Implicit instruction***

language teaching in which learners are not overtly taught linguistic items
Learners' attention is not actively directed to specific language forms.
In an implicit approach to grammar instruction, the teacher does not employ structural analysis or technical terms to explain the linguistic rules. Instead, the target form is used in the utterances made to communicate with the students.

40 Implicit knowledge***

information that is automatically and spontaneously used in language tasks

41 Implicit learning***

learning without awareness of what is being learned
Implicit learning occurs, for example, when a learner sets out to do one thing but learns something else about the language at the same time. (while practicing communication, learning grammatical aspect) It is sometimes confused with *incidental learning* as the learner does not deliberately set out to learn the grammatical aspect of the language. However, with incidental learning, learners may be aware that they are learning something even if it was not their original intention.

42 Implicit (treatment of form)***

incorporation of formal elements of language without focal attention to forms, as opposed to *explicit treatment of form*

43 Incidental learning***

learning that happens <u>without the learner intending for it to occur</u>
For example, learners may be involved in a communicative activity in which they are discussing a specific topic. Thus, primary intention is for them to practise speaking the L2. However, during that activity, a learner may notice and learn a specific lexical item or grammatical structure.
incidental exposure to lexical items <u>as a by-product of communicative activities</u>
<u>Based on sufficient comprehensible input</u>, learners' L2 vocabulary acquisition would largely take care of itself.

44 Inductive approach***

It involves the learners <u>detecting, or noticing, patterns and working out a 'rule' for themselves</u> before they practise the language.

45 Inductive reasoning ⓔ

recalling a number of <u>specific instances in order to induce a general law or rule or conclusion</u> that governs or subsumes the specific instances

46 Input enhancement***

It is a <u>focus on form task</u> in which specific <u>target structures are highlighted</u> for the purpose of implicit instruction. Improving the quality of input via typical input enhancement techniques such as *color-coding, boldfacing, underlining, italicizing, capitalizing, and highlighting* for textual enhancement purposes and oral repetition for aural enhancement purpose.

47 Input flooding***

Flooding with specific forms of the target language in order to draw learners' attention to the input. The expectation is that ample exposure (frequently and repeatedly) to the same target form in the input will make it more salient, and in doing so, will draw learners' attention to the linguistic form.

48 Input processing***

It addresses how learners comprehend utterances and how they make form-meaning connections. The overall aim is to improve learners' intake which is not all input learners are exposed to, but the input learners actually comprehend in terms of *form, function, and meaning.* It is important that the text used for input remain reasonably natural, and that the learners make the necessary connections between form and function in authentic contexts of L2 use.

Learners' principle when processing L2 input;
- **1st (meaning principle):** Learners pay attention to meaning first and only secondarily to form.
- **2nd (first noun principle):** Learners tend to assign subject status to the first noun or pronoun in a sentence/utterance.

Based on these two principles, processing instruction has been proposed as a teaching method to help learners overcome these processing strategies.

49 Intentional learning***

This is the type of learning that learners consciously plan to do. It often involves the learning of specific grammar rules or vocabulary that are focused on in class. Intentional learning contrasts with incidental learning. Intentional learning is generally considered to be faster and more efficient thant incidental learning, particularly when the topic to be learned is explicit information about the L2. However, there are less consensus about the benefits of intentional learning for the development of *implicit L2 knowledge.*

50 Keyword method / technique***

The method is mnemonic. This is a valuable technique used to memorize the meaning behind vocabulary words, is when a person uses what a word sounds like to visualize something memorable that will help them later recall the definition.

51 Lexical approach***

a language teaching method that emphasized the importance of words/vocabulary in SLA

The lexical approach is a way of analysing and teaching language based on the idea that a language is made up of lexical units rather than grammatical structures. The units are words, chunks formed by collocations, and fixed phrases.

> **Ex**
> The phrase 'Rescue attempts are being hampered by bad weather' is a chunk of language, and almost a fixed phrase. It is formed by the collocations 'Rescue' + 'attempt', 'rescue attempt' + 'hampered', 'hampered' + 'by', 'hampered by' + 'bad weather'.

* **In the classroom**

A simple activity to incorporate the lexical approach is to encourage learners to identify and record lexical chunks and fixed phrases in texts they read.

52 Lexicogrammatical approach***

A view that lexis and grammar are two inherently connected parts of a single entity and should not be treated separately. "Vocabulary and grammatical structures are interdependent; so much so that it is possible to say with some justification that words have their own grammar." This interdependency of lexis and grammar is evident everywhere in language. For example, lexical verbs have valency (v+sth) patterns: some verbs can be used with a direct object, or with both a direct object and an indirect object, others need no object at all.

53　Local error(s)***

errors that do not prevent a message from being understood, usually due to a minor violation of one segment of a sentence, allowing the hearer/reader to make an accurate guess about the intended meaning

54　Meaningful drill(s)***

techniques with a predicted or a limited set of possible responses relating to some form of reality

55　Mechanical drill(s)***

techniques that require only one correct response from a student without connection with reality

56　PPP (presentation, practice, production)***

a method of language instruction that involves the explicit presentation of specific linguistic forms, such as vocabulary items or grammar rules
PPP is often associated with more traditional types of L2 instruction, in which the target language is presented in a largely decontextualized, non-communicative context. This presentation is followed by controlled learner practice of the target forms. Finally, freer production is using the forms is allowed. PPP has been criticized because it does not take into account learners' order of development, nor does it allow learners to use the language items for primarily communicative purposes.

57　Procedural knowledge***

It is knowledge of how to do something. This enables a student to apply a rule of grammar in communication.

58 Processing instruction***

a type of language teaching based on Bill Vanpattern's input processing theory, which argues that learners use certain processing strategy to understand the L2
Processing instruction is entirely comprehension-based. Learners are given target language input but are not required to produce it.

59 Productive knowledge***

the type of knowledge that learners can use to produce language
It is typically used to refer to vocabulary knowledge and contrasts with receptive knowledge. Learners' productive vocabulary knowledge is generally smaller than their receptive knowledge.

60 Receptive knowledge***

the ability of learners to understand what is said to them even if they are not able to produce a comparable utterance
There term is particularly used with *vocabulary knowledge* when learners know the meaning of a word they hear, but they would not be able to come up with the word on their own. It is generally accepted that learners' receptive knowledge of vocabulary is greater than their productive knowledge. Receptive knowledge is also sometimes referred to as *passive knowledge.*

61 Restructuring***

the process by which a learner's internal grammar changes and develops
Learning therefore involves bringing new information into the learner's interlanguage system and reordering that system. Restructuring does not merely consist of the addition of new information, but rather involves making changes to the pre-existing system.

62   Salience***

It refers to how noticeable (or explicit) a linguistic structure is in the input. Some researchers argue that learners must notice L2 structures before they can learn them; therefore, more salient structures may be more easily learned because they are more noticeable. There are several different ways in which salience increases. First, it is possible that **frequency** may affect saliency, with structures with either very high or very low frequency being more salient. Second, salience can increase through enhancing the form of the input either through the manipulation of written or spoken structures. This might take the shape of bolding, underlining words in a passage or giving extra stress or emphasis to a spoken form. The relative size of a structure and its meaning load may also be a factor. Lexical words, such as *dog* and *cat*, that carry essential meaning may be more salient than function words, such as *and* and *in*.

63   Structured input***

a type of language that has been modified to draw learners' attention to specific linguistic forms
It is most frequently related to processing instruction, a method of language teaching that provides learners with language that has been manipulated to draw learners' attention to the fact that they may be relying on a strategy for processing language that does not work in the target language. Thus, it might contain language that cannot be understood correctly by using L1 strategies. (**Ex** to determine subjects and objects in a sentence, learners must rely on word order in English, but the conjugations of the verbs in Spanish)

64   Structured input activities***

Structured input activities ensure that L2 learners simultaneously focus on form to obtain the meaning of the sentence they are exposed to, so that they improve their ability to process the right information and make the right form-meaning connections during comprehension.

> **Ex**
> *** Types of structured input activities**
> · Supplying information
> · Surveys
> · Matching
> · Binary options (True/false, Logical/illogical, etc)
> · Ordering / Ranking
> · Selecting alternatives

65 Structured output***

In terms of progression, structured output activities should follow structured input activities.

Lee and VanPatten define structured output as "a special type of form-focused activity that is communicative in nature" (2003: 168). They provide two major characteristics of structured output activities:

(a) They involve the exchange of previously unknown information.

(b) They require learners to access a particular form or structure in order to express meaning.

The guidelines established by Lee and Van Patten for developing structured output activities include:

* Present one thing at a time.

* Keep meaning in focus.

* Move from sentences to connected discourse.

* Use both oral and written output.

* Others must respond to the content of the output.

* The learner must have some knowledge of the form or structure.

66 Teachability hypothesis***

Manfred Pienemann proposed that in order for linguistic structures to be learned, they must be relatively close to a learner's current interlanguage status. Structures they are too far beyond the learner's interlanguage are not teachable. Thus, he argued that the linguistic structures that are taught in the L2 classroom should follow the learner's stages of acquisition. However, there are some difficulties with such a proposal: (a) the stages of acquisition are known for only a limited number of linguistic structures in only a few languages (b) learners within the same class may be at different stages of acquisition.

67 Vocabulary analysis (=word analysis)***

(a) Look for prefixes (co–, inter–, un–, etc.) that may give a clue.
(b) Look for suffixes (–tion, –tive, –ally, etc.) that may indicate what part of speech it is.
(c) Look for roots that are familiar. (Ex) 'intervening' may be a word that a student doesn't know, but recognizing that the root 'ven' comes from Latin 'to come' would yield the meaning 'to come in between')

08

68 Word family(ies)***

A word family is the base form of a word plus its inflected forms and derived forms made with suffixes and prefixes plus its cognates. (e.g. wrought(iron) and work(ed))
The idea is that a base word and its inflected forms support the same meaning, and can be considered learned words if a learner knows both the base word and the affix.

<Guideline>
· Introduce derivatives along with their roots.
· Teach more affixes.
· Emphasize adverbs, adjectives, and their derivations.
· Suggest reading that includes those word families.

69 Word formation***

Word formation is the process by which <u>new words are formed by</u> adding an affix, another word or converting from one word class to another by removing and adding alphabets. *Derivation* is the most common process of word formation. Derivation is accomplished when affixes (suffixes and prefixes) are added to words. Examples of derivatives: 'dis- + respect + -ful = disrespectful', 'care + -less = careless'.

70 Word-learning strategies ®

some word-attack strategies

(a) <u>word building</u> (based on *suffixes, prefixes, roots*)

(b) definition clues (based on *synonyms, antonyms* or *superordinates* within the sentences, and given definitions within parentheses)

(c) <u>inference clues</u>
- *specific*: Peru is trying to restore some of its deteriorated *monuments*. *Machu Picchu* is being partly rebuilt by curators.
- *restatement*: Some products are designed to stop *perspiration*, but this *bodily secretion of salty liquid* can actually help to cool you.
- *contextual cues*: The old dog *snuffled* and *moped* as he *sadly walked* from room to room.

(d) <u>word associations</u>
- linking meaning: fat pig, tall tree
- collocations: tell the truth, make a copy

71 Word map***

There are many different variations on how to use this strategy. One way is to use the four-corner vocabulary chart, and with this method, students write the definition, use it in a sentence, draw a picture of the word, and write the word in the corner. Other methods to use this strategy are to <u>add antonyms, synonyms, dictionary definitions, part of speech and more</u>. This strategy can be adjusted to meet the needs of all learners.

※ **Read the following descriptions and fill in the blanks.**

01 _____ **approach**

It involves the learners understanding hidden rules of language use through the process of exploring hypotheses and inferences.

Abduction refers to the exploratory process of trying out tentative solutions to problems or facts to figure out what may happen, to see if they work, or to experience something new. (Cunningham, 2002) Language teachers can start with abduction, taking experiential and exploratory approaches (**Ex** puzzle-based learning) and then move on to either inductive or deductive tasks as relevant, followed with further exploration at a wider or deeper level.

02 _____

Using appropriate language means that a speaker's language is suitable or fitting for themselves, as the speaker; our audience; the speaking context; and the speech itself. Students need to know if a particular lexical item is usually used in writing or in speech; or in formal or informal discourse.

03 _____ _____ _____

This term is used primarily in vocabulary acquisition to refer to the size of a learner's vocabulary. It is concerned with the number of words that a learner knows, either productively or receptively. As such, the term contrasts with depth of knowledge, which refers to how much learners know about specific words. Some researchers argue that knowledge of the 3,000 most common words in a language will enable a learner to study in that language with relative ease.

04 _____

THIS is a group of words that often occur together. For example, in English one 'plays tennis' but 'goes skiing'. There are often no fixed rules for THIS and THIS is often one of the last components of vocabulary that L2 learners learn.

05 _____

(a) THIS refers to language production that expresses multiple ideas within a sentence by using subordination. In this sense, it is one way to measure a language learner's ability in the second language in addition to fluency and accuracy.

(b) THIS is a measure of the degree to which an activity involving language requires greater amounts of mental effort and attention. THIS can be varied by task designers, for example by asking learners to pay attention to more than one feature in a task.

(c) the lexical variety and syntactic elaborateness of the learner's linguistic system

(d) (related to reading skills) The linguistic differences between speech and writing are one of major contributing cause to difficulty. Writing and speech represent different modes of THIS, and the most salient difference is in the nature of clauses. Spoken language tends to have shorter clauses connected by more coordinate conjunctions, while writing has longer clauses and more subordination. The shorter clauses are often a factor of the **redundancy** we build into speech (repeating subjects and verbs for clarity).

> **Ex**
>
> The cognitive THIS of versions (1) and (2) are not different. But structurally, four sentences were used in version (b) to replace the one lone sentence of version (a).
>
> (1) Because of the frequent ambiguity that therefore is present in a good deal of writing, readers must do their best to infer, to interpret, and to "read between the lines". (Written version)
>
> (2) There's frequent ambiguity in a lot of writing. And so, readers have to infer a lot. They also have to interpret what they read. And sometimes they have to "read between the lines". (Spoken version)

(e) (related to writing skills) Writers must learn the discourse features of written L2, how to create syntactic and lexical variety, how to combine sentences, and more. Sentence combining can pose some difficulty for learners of English. Learning to use coordinating and subordinating clauses effectively in writing poses a challenge even for native English users.

06 _____

It is an alphabetical list of the principal words used in a book or body of work, listing every instance of each word with its immediate context. The sample of THIS can provide students with instances of real language use helping learners to know how to use language that is appropriate in different contexts.

07 _____

THIS is a computer program that automatically constructs a concordance.

08 _____

indexing of words that enables one to reference words in the multiple possible contexts in which they appear in spoken or written language consciousness-raising, drawing students' attention to formal elements of language within the context of meaningful communication and tasks

THIS allows learners to see words in context, while the extensive corpora serve as databanks that facilitate a deeper examination and understanding of the relationships between grammatical and lexical units.

09 _____

THIS of a word is <u>the emotional or positive-negative associations</u> that is implies. A closely related word is implication.

10 _____ **task (CR task)**

A task that involves inductively drawing learners' attention to characteristics of the target language. As such, <u>they do not aim to enable learners to produce the target form</u>; instead, the goals is for learners to <u>become aware of specific</u> L2 characteristics so that <u>they can notice them in the input</u>. An example of a CR task would be to provide learners with a group of sentences that contain examples of a specific rule. Learners would <u>induce the rule by looking at the sentences and then writing out the rule after they have identified it</u>. Ellis et al. (2001) define THIS as a pedagogic activity where the learners are provided with second language data in some form and required to perform some operation on it, the purpose of which is to arrive at an explicit understanding of the target grammar. THIS seems to be similar to the PPP (presentation, practice, production) model, but one significant difference is clear. In the PPP model, students are required to use a target form in speaking or writing. However, in THIS, what learners should be able to do is not to use the form in speaking and writing but to find the rule and understand the target form in terms of form, meaning, and function.

11 _____

plural of corpus

12 _____ **knowledge**

knowledge about something
Consciously known and <u>verbalizable facts, knowledge, and information</u>. This enables a student to describe a rule of grammar and apply it in pattern practice drills.

13 _____ **approach**

It involves the learners being given a general rule, which is then applied to specific language examples and honed through practice exercises.

14 _____ _____ _____

a term, primarily associated with vocabulary learning, that describes the amount of information that a learner knows about a specific word

Learners may only know the basis form and meaning of a word, or they may have a deeper knowledge of the word, such as its *derivational forms,* its *collocations or its connotations.* (**Ex** knowing the verb *break*, and also *take a break* and *break up*)

08

15 _____

a variation on the dictocomp technique

It is a task-based procedure designed to help L2 learners internalize certain grammatical elements that are built into a text. Through the reconstruction of a text, students come to notice certain grammatical features. Before the reconstruction stage, students are not asked to notice a grammatical form, even though they are embedded in the text. Only at the last stage of the procedure will students possibly become aware of using the form.

16 _____

a mechanical technique focusing on a minimal number of language forms through repetition

THIS offers students an opportunity to listen and to orally repeat certain strings of language that may pose some linguistic difficulty - either phonological or grammatical. They allow students to focus on one element of language in a controlled activity.

<Guidelines>
· Keep them simple (just one point at a time).
· Keep them short (a few minutes of a class hour).
· Limit them to phonological, morphological, or syntactic points.
· Make sure they ultimately lead to communicative goals.

17 _____ **instruction**

language teaching that draws attention to language items and language rules in a clear manner and with the express purpose of teaching those linguistic items and rules

THIS involves the overt presentation of rules of the L2. This can be done both deductively and inductively.

18 _____ _____ _____

an approach that attempts to induce learners' incidental learning by drawing their attention to target forms while they are engaged in communicative activities

19 _____ _____ _____

THIS involves more traditional approaches to grammar that consist of isolating individual linguistic constructs out of context. ("the use of some kind of synthetic syllabus and/or a linguistically isolating teaching method, such as audiolingualism, the Silent Way, or Total Physical Response")

20 _____ _____ _____

THIS does not allow for any attention whatsoever to the linguistic code of the L2. The assumption behind this approach is that an L2 is learned best by allowing students to experience the L2 through communication and not through rigorous study. (Ex Krashen's Natural Approach, immersion programs)

21 _____ _____

any pedagogical effort used to draw a learner's attention to language form either implicitly or explicitly
A range of instructional methods that direct learners' attention to language items. As such, THIS contrasts with meaning-focused instruction. It is generally divided into two main categories: *focus on forms* (Ex grammar translation and PPP) and *focus on form* (Ex input flood and input enhancement).

22 _____

the number of times that a linguistic item occurs in either input or output, in a given amount of time
Various researchers have asserted that learners should receive explicit instruction and practice for the first two to three thousand *High* _____ *words* and beyond this threshold level, most *Low* _____ *words* will be learned implicitly while reading or listening. The reason is that it is very difficult to guess the meaning of new words unless many words on a page are known.

23 _____ _____

THIS is the most explicit technique. A teacher takes learners into making overgeneralization regarding a grammatical rule so that the learners can notice the form more impressively. That is, when a teacher plans to teach a certain target form, the teacher only briefly explains the major rules of the form instead of its exceptions. Then, the teacher corrects students' errors, providing the rule of the exceptions when students' overgeneralization actually occur.

24 _____ _____

errors that <u>hinder communication</u> or prevent a hearer (or reader) from comprehending some aspect of a message

25 _____

conforming to <u>the systematic use</u> of the target language
L1 speakers do not always agree in what they feel is grammatical due to regional variation or feelings related to socially acceptable forms of the language.

26 _____

a phenomenon in which language speakers <u>overuses language rules in contexts</u> where they do not apply
A speaker or writer who produces THIS generally believes <u>through a misunderstanding of such rules that the form is more "correct"</u>, standard, or otherwise preferable, often combined with <u>a desire to appear formal or educated</u>. For example, the correction of the subject-positioned "you and me" to "you and I" leads people to "internalize the rule that 'you and I' is somehow more proper, and they end up using it in places where they should not – such as 'he gave it to you and I' when it should be 'he gave it to you and me.'" Often, the linguistic form being overused in seen as being socially more prestigious.

27 _____ **instruction**

language teaching in which learners are <u>not overtly taught</u> linguistic items
Learners' attention is not actively directed to <u>specific language forms</u>.
In THIS approach to grammar instruction, the teacher does <u>not</u> employ structural analysis or technical <u>terms to explain</u> the linguistic rules. Instead, <u>the target form is used</u> in the utterances made <u>to communicate with the students</u>.

28 _____ **knowledge**

information that is <u>automatically and spontaneously used</u> in language tasks

29 _____ **learning**

learning that happens <u>without the learner intending for it to occur</u>
For example, learners may be involved in a communicative activity in which they are discussing a specific topic. Thus, primary intention is for them to practise speaking the L2. However, during that activity, a learner may notice and learn a specific lexical item or grammatical structure.
incidental exposure to lexical items <u>as a by-product of communicative activities</u>
Based on <u>sufficient comprehensible input</u>, learners' L2 vocabulary acquisition would largely take care of itself.

08

30 _____ **approach**

It involves the learners <u>detecting, or noticing, patterns and working out</u> a 'rule' <u>for themselves</u> before they practise the language.

31 _____ _____

It is a <u>focus on form</u> task in which specific <u>target structures are highlighted</u> for the purpose of implicit instruction. Improving the quality of input via typical THIS techniques such as *color-coding, boldfacing, underlining, italicizing, capitalizing, and highlighting* for textual enhancement purposes and oral repetition for aural enhancement purpose.

32 _____ _____

Flooding with specific forms of the target language in order to draw learners' attention to the input. The expectation is that <u>ample exposure</u> (frequently and repeatedly) to the same target form in the input will make it more salient, and in doing so, will draw learners' attention to the linguistic form.

33 _____ _____

It addresses how learners comprehend utterances and how they make <u>form-meaning connections</u>. The overall aim is <u>to improve learners' intake</u> which is not all input learners are exposed to, but <u>the input learners actually comprehend</u> in terms of *form*, *function*, and *meaning*. It is important that the text used for input remain reasonably natural, and that the learners <u>make the necessary connections between form and function</u> in authentic contexts of L2 use.

> **Cf**
> Learners' principle when processing L2 input;
> · **1st (meaning principle)**: Learners pay attention to meaning first and only secondarily to form.
> · **2nd (first noun principle)**: Learners tend to assign subject status to the first noun or pronoun in a sentence/utterance.
> Based on these two principles, processing instruction has been proposed as a teaching method to help learners overcome these processing strategies.

34 _____ _____ / _____

The method is <u>mnemonic</u>. This is a valuable technique used to <u>memorize the meaning</u> behind vocabulary words, is when a person uses <u>what a word sounds like</u> to <u>visualize something memorable</u> that will help them later recall the definition.

35 _____ _____

errors that <u>do not prevent a message from being understood</u>, usually due to a <u>minor violation</u> of one segment of a sentence, allowing the hearer/reader to make an accurate guess about the intended meaning

36 _____ _____

techniques with <u>a predicted or a limited set of possible responses</u> relating to <u>some form of reality</u>

37 _____ _____

techniques that require <u>only one correct response</u> from a student <u>without connection with reality</u>

38 _____ **(presentation, practice, production)**

a method of language instruction that involves the explicit presentation of specific linguistic forms, such as vocabulary items or grammar rules
THIS is often associated with more traditional types of L2 instruction, in which the target language is presented in a largely decontextualized, non-communicative context. This presentation is followed by controlled learner practice of the target forms. Finally, freer production is using the forms is allowed. THIS has been criticized because it does not take into account learners' order of development, nor does it allow learners to use the language items for primarily communicative purposes.

39 _____ **knowledge**

It is knowledge of how to do something. This enables a student to <u>apply a rule</u> of grammar in communication.

40 _____ **knowledge**

the type of knowledge that learners can use to produce language
It is typically used to refer to <u>vocabulary knowledge</u> and <u>contrasts with receptive knowledge</u>. Learners' productive vocabulary knowledge is generally smaller than their receptive knowledge.

41 _____ **knowledge**

the ability of learners to <u>understand what is said</u> to them even if they are <u>not able to produce</u> a comparable utterance
The term is particularly used with *vocabulary knowledge* when learners know the meaning of a word they hear, but they would not be able to come up with the word on their own. It is generally accepted that learners' THIS knowledge of vocabulary is greater than their productive knowledge. THIS knowledge is also sometimes referred to as *passive knowledge*.

42 _____

the process by which a learner's <u>internal grammar changes and develops</u>
Learning therefore involves bringing new information into the learner's interlanguage system and reordering that system. THIS does not merely consist of the addition of new information, but rather involves making changes to the pre-existing system.

43 _____ _____

a type of language that has been <u>modified to draw learners' attention</u> to specific linguistic forms

It is most frequently related to processing instruction, a method of language teaching that provides learners with language that has been manipulated to draw learners' attention to the fact that they may be <u>relying on a strategy for processing language</u> that does not work in the target language. Thus, it might contain language that cannot be understood correctly by using L1 strategies. (Ex. to determine subjects and objects in a sentence, learners must rely on word order in English, but the conjugations of the verbs in Spanish)

44 _____ _____

Manfred Pienemann proposed that in order for linguistic structures to be learned, they must be relatively close to <u>a learner's current interlanguage status.</u> Structures they are too far beyond the learner's interlanguage are not teachable. Thus, he argued that the linguistic structures that are taught in the L2 classroom <u>should follow the learner's stages of acquisition</u>. However, there are some difficulties with such a proposal: (a) the stages of acquisition are known for only a limited number of linguistic structures in only a few languages (b) learners within the same class may be at different stages of acquisition.

45 _____ _____

(a) Look for prefixes (co–, inter–, un–, etc.) that may give a clue.
(b) Look for suffixes (–tion, –tive, –ally, etc.) that may indicate what part of speech it is.
(c) Look for roots that are familiar. (**Ex** 'intervening' may be a word that a student doesn't know, but recognizing that the root 'ven' comes from Latin 'to come' would yield the meaning 'to come in between')

46 _____   _____

THIS is the process by which <u>new words are formed by</u> adding an affix, another word or converting from one word class to another by removing and adding alphabets. *Derivation* is the most common process of THIS. Derivation is accomplished when affixes (suffixes and prefixes) are added to words. Examples of derivatives: 'dis- + respect + -ful = disrespectful', 'care + -less = careless'.

47 _____   _____

There are many different variations on how to use this strategy. One way is to use the four-corner vocabulary chart, and with this method, students write the definition, use it in a sentence, draw a picture of the word, and write the word in the corner. Other methods to use this strategy are to <u>add antonyms, synonyms, dictionary definitions, part of speech and more</u>. This strategy can be adjusted to meet the needs of all learners.

Answers

01 Abductive	20 Focus on meaning
02 Appropriateness	21 Form-focused instruction
03 Breadth of knowledge	22 Frequency
04 Collocation	23 Garden path
05 Complexity	24 Global errors
06 Concordance	25 Grammaticality
07 Concordancer	26 Hypercorrection
08 Concordancing	27 Implicit
09 Connotation	28 Implicit
10 Consciousness-raising	29 Incidental
11 Corpora	30 Inductive
12 Declarative	31 Input enhancement
13 Deductive	32 Input flooding
14 Depth of knowledge	33 Input processing
15 Dictogloss	34 Keyword method / techique
16 Drill	35 Local errors
17 Explicit	36 Meaningful drills
18 Focus on form	37 Mechanical drills
19 Focus on forms	38 PPP

39 Procedural

40 Productive

41 Receptive

42 Restructuring

43 Structured input

44 Teachability hypothesis

45 Vocabulary analysis

46 Word formation

47 Word map

Note

Chapter

09

Assessment & Test

KEYTERM MASTER

for EFL teachers

※ **Review the following Key Terms list and put a checkmark next to Terms that you do not know the exact meaning.**

☐ Achievement test

☐ Alternative assessment

☐ Analytic scoring method

☐ Appropriate word scoring (acceptable word method)

☐ Assessment

☐ Authentic assessment

☐ Authenticity

☐ Classroom-based assessment

☐ Cloze test

☐ Communicative language test

☐ Concurrent validity

☐ Construct validity

☐ Content validity

☐ Criterion validity

☐ Criterion-referenced test

☐ Critical language assessment

☐ C-test

☐ Diagnostic test

☐ Direct test

☐ Discrete point testing

☐ Distractor (efficiency) analysis

☐ Electronic portfolio (e-portfolio)

☐ Exact word method

☐ Face validity

☐ Fixed-ratio deletion

☐ Formal assessment

☐ Formative assessment/test

- ☐ High stakes
- ☐ Holistic scoring method
- ☐ Indirect test
- ☐ Informal assessment
- ☐ Integrative testing
- ☐ Internal consistency
- ☐ Inter-rater reliability
- ☐ Intra-rater reliability
- ☐ Item difficulty
- ☐ Item discrimination
- ☐ Item facility
- ☐ Journals
- ☐ Norm-referenced test
- ☐ Objective test
- ☐ Performance assessment
- ☐ Placement test
- ☐ Portfolio(s)
- ☐ Practicality
- ☐ Predictive validity
- ☐ Proficiency test
- ☐ Rational deletion
- ☐ Reliability
- ☐ Rubrics
- ☐ Self- and peer- assessment
- ☐ Student-related reliability
- ☐ Subjective test
- ☐ Summative assessment / test
- ☐ Test
- ☐ Test relibility
- ☐ Validity
- ☐ Washback

01 Achievement test***

The purpose of THIS is to determine whether course objectives have been met with skills acquired by the end of a period of instruction. THIS should be limited to particular material addressed in a curriculum within a particular time frame. THIS belongs to summative because they are administered at the end of a unit/term of study. It analyzes the extent to which students have acquired language that has already been taught.

02 Alternative assessment (e.g. portfolios, journals, self- and peer-assessment)***

THIS is a method of evaluation that measures a student's level of proficiency in a subject as opposed to the student's level of knowledge. The overall goal of alternative assessment is to allow students to demonstrate their knowledge and execute tasks.

03 Analytic scoring method***

For classroom instruction, holistic scoring provides little washback into the writer's / speaker's further stages of learning. Classroom evaluation of learning is best served through analytic scoring, in which as many as major elements of writing / speaking are scored, thus enabling learners to capture their weaknesses and strengths.

04 Appropriate word scoring (acceptable word method) (in Cloze test)***

It credits the test-taker for supplying any word that is grammatically correct and that makes good sense in the context.

05   Assessment ©

an <u>ongoing process</u> ranging from formal tests to informal evaluation
Evaluating the L2 proficiency level of a learner. Ranging from <u>very informal to highly</u>
<u>standardized</u>. One important issue related to assessment is the content that is being
evaluated. (**Ex**) learners' grammatical ability, spoken language, communicative ability,
writing ability, etc) When choosing a test for assessment purposes, it is important to
<u>consider the goal</u> of the testing process. If learners are being evaluated for their general
communication skills, then it is necessary for the test to measure those skills, rather
than focusing on grammatical ability, or some other area of langauge that is less directly
related to communicative ability. (see also **Test**)

06   Authentic assessment***

THIS is a form of assessment in which students are asked to <u>perform real-world tasks</u>
that demonstrate meaningful application of essential knowledge and skills. Authentic
assessment engages students in applying knowledge and skills in the same way they are
used in the "real world" outside school. It is <u>performance-based assessment</u> that requires
a student to go <u>beyond basic recall</u> and demonstrate significant, worthwhile knowledge
and understanding through a product, performance or exhibition. The assessment
comprises <u>an authentic task</u> such as *participating in politically oriented debates, writing*
for the school newspaper, conduct a research group meeting or perform scientific
research.

07   Authenticity (of a test)***

the degree of correspondence of the characteristics of a given language test task to the
features of a target language task
Essentially, when you make a claim for authenticity in a test task, you are saying that
this <u>task is likely to be enacted in the "real world."</u>

> **Ex**
> * **Criteria for designing an authentic test**
> · The language in the test is as natural as possible.
> · Items are contextualized rather than isolated. (multiple-choice items)
> · Topics and situations are interesting, enjoyable, and humorous.
> · Thematic organization to items is provided. (**Ex** through a storyline)
> · Tasks represent, or closely approximate, real-world tasks.

08 Classroom-based assessment [B]

instruments either created or adapted to assess classroom/course objectives (as opposed to standardized, large-scale testing)

09 Cloze test***

In written language, a sentence with a word left out should have enough context that a reader can close that gap with a calculated guess, using linguistic expectancies (formal schemata), back-ground experience (content schemata), and some strategic competence.

10 Communicative language test [E]

assessment that incorporates authentic, meaningful, real-world tasks

11 Concurrent validity***

The extent of the agreement between two measures or assessments taken at the same time. It compares a new assessment with one that has already been tested and proven to be valid. (a subtype of **criterion validity**)
A test has concurrent validity if its results are supported by other concurrent performance.

Ex If the new test results correlate with the existing validated measure, concurrent validity can be established.

12   Construct validity***

the extent to which a test actually taps into the theoretical construct that it proposes to assess
"Proficiency" and "communicative competence" are a linguistic construct. ("Does this test actually tap into the theoretical construct as it has been defined?")

13   Content validity***

If a test actually samples the subject matter about which conclusions are to be drawn, and if it requires the test-taker to perform the behavior that is being measured, it can claim *content-related evidence* of validity, often popularly referred to as content validity.

14   Criterion validity***

the extent to which the "criterion" of the test has actually been reached
In the case of teacher-made classroom assessments, *criterion-related evidence* is best demonstrated through a comparison of results of an assessment with results of some other measure of the same criterion.(**Ex** concurrent validity, predictive validity)

15   Criterion-referenced test***

This occurs when candidates are measured against defined (and objective) criteria. It is designed to give test-takers feedback on specific course or lesson objectives.

16 Critical language assessment Ⓔ

the recognition that <u>tests represent a social technology</u> deeply embedded in education, government, and business, and as such, they provide the mechanism for <u>enforcing power and control</u>
Tests are most powerful as they are often <u>the single indicators for determining the future of individuals.</u> (Shohamy, 1997) Test designers have an obligation to maintain certain standards as specified by their client educational institutions. These standards bring with them certain <u>ethical issues</u> surrounding the *gate-keeping* nature of high-stakes standardized test (Ross, 2011).

17 C-test (related to Cloze test)***

<u>The second half</u> (according to the number of letters) <u>of every other word is obliterated,</u> and the test-taker must restore each word.

18 Diagnostic test***

an assessment instrument designed to <u>analyze a test-taker's strengths and weaknesses</u> in terms of grammar, pronunciation, fluency, discourse, or other targeted linguistic features
The test offers a checklist of features for the teacher to use in discovering difficulties. This test will typically <u>offer more detailed sub-categorized information</u> on the learner.

19 Direct test***

Testing involves the test-taker in <u>actually performing</u> the target task.

20 Discrete point testing (e.g., multiple-choice, grammar item)***

assessment on the assumption that language could be broken down <u>into its component parts and those parts adequately tested</u>

Language is segmented into many small linguistic points and the four language skills of listening, speaking, reading and writing. Test questions are designed to test these skills and linguistic points.

21 Distractor (efficiency) analysis***

Analyzing the distractors (i.e., incorrect alternatives) is useful in determining the relative usefulness of the decoys in each item.

22 Electronic portfolio (e-portfolio)***

(also known as a digital portfolio, online portfolio, e-portfolio, e-folio, or eFolio)
Electronic portfolio is a collection of electronic evidence assembled and managed by a user, usually but not only on the Web (online portfolio).
Such electronic evidence may include input text, electronic files, images, multimedia, blog entries, and hyperlinks. E-portfolios are both demonstrations of the user's abilities and platforms for self-expression. If they are online, users can maintain them dynamically over time. E-portfolios, like traditional portfolios, can facilitate students' reflection on their own learning, leading to more awareness of learning strategies and needs.

23 Exact word method (in Cloze test)***

Students get credit for a correct answer if and only if the word they write in any given blank is the exact word deleted from the original text. This is approach is quick and, therefore, very practical, and also highly reliable.

24 Face validity***

the extent to which a test, on the "face" of it, appears from the learner's perspective to test what it is designed to test

25 Fixed-ratio deletion (in Cloze test)***

Typically every seventh word (plus or minus two) is deleted.

26 Formal assessment***

deliberate, planned assessment using scoring and grading criteria and usually with conventionalized feedback
systematic, planned sampling techniques to assess students' achievement
It has conventionalized feedback.
All tests are formal assessments, but not all formal assessments is testing.
Ex exercises, or procedures specifically designed to tap into skills and knowledge

27 Formative assessment / test***

ongoing informal evaluation serving the purpose of facilitating improvement in a student's performance
In an educational setting, formative assessment might be a teacher (or peer) or the learner providing feedback on a student's work, and would not necessarily be used for grading purposes. Formative assessment is diagnostic.
It helps students to "check" progress, to discern areas that need improvement, and to give them some future goals to pursue.

28 High stakes (standardized tests) ©

instruments used to make crucial decisions about one's future path (**Ex** college entrance, employment, certification)

29 Holistic scoring method***

Uses a rubric for scoring (spoken / written) production holistically. Each point on a holistic scale is given a systematic set of descriptors, and the reader-evaluator matches an overall impression with the descriptors to arrive at a score.

30 Indirect test***

In this test, learners are not performing the task itself but rather a task that is related in some way.

31 Informal assessment***

incidental, unplanned evaluation usually embedded in classroom tasks, and usually designed to elicit improved performance (see also **formal assessment**)
Usually, it has no specific scoring or grading formats.
(Ex teacher's incidental, unplanned comments and responses like Nice job! Did you say can or can't? You 'go' to the movies yesterday? or a marginal comment on a paper)

32 Integrative testing (e.g., interviews, Cloze test)***

This attempts to assess a learner's capacity to use many bits all at the same time, and possibly while exercising several presumed components of a grammatical system, and perhaps more than one of the traditional skills or aspects of skills.

33 Internal consistency (reliability)***

Internal consistency reliability looks at each item in a test that measures the same content. It assesses the correlation between multiple items in a test that are intended to measure the same construct. Internal consistency reliability is a type of reliability used to determine the validity of similar items on a test. All questions on a test proposed to measure certain content should produce similar and consistent results. Researchers use internal consistency reliability to ensure that each item on a test is related to the topic they are researching. Ensuring items on a test are relevant to the study and measuring the same construct ensures that the test is valid. As a result, other researchers can depend on the results. Not having consistent reliability in a study renders the test results invalid. A test without internal consistency reliability could create questionable results that may not create usable data. The three measures are *Cronbach's Alpha, split-half test, and Kuder-Richardson test.* As one example, Cronbach's Alpha has a range of 0-1. The closer to 1, the more reliable the assessment. The scale determines how much agreement each item in a test has. The more agreement, the more the question are aligned or alike. The scale is as follows:
* **0.00-0.69** = Poor alignment
* **0.70-0.79** = Fair alignment
* **0.80-0.89** = Good alignment
* **0.90-0.99** = Excellent/strong alignment

34 Inter-rater reliability***

Human error, subjectivity, and bias may enter into the scoring process. THIS occurs when two or more scorers yield inconsistent scores of the same test, possibly for lack of attention to scoring criteria, inexperience, inattention, or even preconceived biases. In the story above about the placement test, the initial scoring plan for the dictations was found to be unreliable- that is, the two scorers were not applying the same standards.

35 Intra-rater reliability***

the degree of agreement among repeated administrations of a diagnostic test performed by a single rater

36   Item difficulty***

see also **Item facility**

37   Item discrimination***

the extent to which <u>an item differentiates between high-and low-ability test-takers</u>. If a test is given to a large group of people, the discriminating power of an item can be measured by <u>comparing the number of people with high test scores who answered that item correctly with the number of people with low scores who answered the same item correctly</u>. If a particular item is doing a good job of discriminating between those who score high and those who score low, more people in the top-scoring group will have answered the item correctly. ($-1 <$ ID < 1) Items with a ID of ≥ 0.35 were considered excellent, those between $0.2 - 0.34$ were considered acceptable and those < 0.2 were considered poor.

38   Item facility (=item difficulty)***

This is the extent to which <u>an item is easy or difficult</u> for the proposed group of test-takers.
* **P** = The number of correct responses divided by the number of total test takers
* **0** = difficult item, **1** = easy item

39   Journals***

This is a log (or "account") of one's thoughts, feelings, reactions, assessments, ideas, or progress toward goals, <u>usually written with little attention to structure, form, or correctness</u>. Learners can articulate their thoughts without the threat of those thoughts being judged later (usually by the teacher).

40   Norm-referenced test***

instrument in which each test-taker's score is interpreted in relation to a mean, median, standard deviation, and/or percentile rank

41   Objective test (e.g., multiple-choice, true or false answers, matching questions)***

This is a form of questioning that has a single correct answer.

42   Performance assessment (performance-based assessment)***

An approach to educational assessment that requires students to directly demonstrate what they know and are able to do through open-ended tasks such as *constructing an answer, producing a project, or performing an activity*. It is a form of testing that requires students to perform a task rather than select an answer from a ready-made list. For example, a student may be asked to generate scientific hypothesis, solve mathematics problems, converse in foreign language. The modes include: *open-ended or extended response exercise; extended tasks; and portfolio*s, teacher observation, oral presentations, hands-on problems, real world simulation *and other authentic tasks*. Advocates said that performance assessment may be a more valued indicator of what students know and what he is able to do (knowledge & abilities) promotes active learning and curricula-based testing.

43   Placement test***

The purpose of THIS is to place a student into a particular level or section of a language curriculum or school. It usually includes a sampling of the material to be covered in the various courses in a curriculum. That is, it has content validity. A student's performance on the test should indicate the point at which the student will find material neither too easy nor too difficult.

44   Portfolio(s)***

a purposeful collection of students' work that demonstrates ... their efforts, progress, and achievements in given areas

This includes materials such as... *essays and compositions in draft and final forms; reports, project outlines; artwork, photos, newspaper or magazine clippings; audio and/or video recordings of presentations, demonstrations, etc.; self and peer-assessments.* The term 'portfolio' is used to describe an instrument for recording progress (process) and ability (product) in the target language. This could be as simple as a pen and paper notebook, or as extensive as a computer-based record-keeping tool. Portfolios can be used to support learning by encouraging learners to reflect on the language learning process, to record experiences in using the language, and get motivation based on their achievement recorded. Portfolios are often used as learning or teaching aids in learner-centered approaches to encourage critical reflection and to give some degree of control over the learning process to the language learner.

45   Practicality***

the extent to which an instrument is within desirable financial limitations, time constraints, and ease of administration, scoring, and interpretation

A prohibitively expensive test is impractical. A test of language proficiency that takes a student five hours to complete is impractical – it consumes more time (and money) than necessary to accomplish its objective.

46   Predictive validity***

the capacity of an assessment to predict future performance

Predictive validity of an assessment becomes important in the case of placement tests, admissions assessment batteries, language aptitude tests, and the like. The assessment criterion in such cases is not to measure concurrent ability but to assess (and predict) a test-taker's likelihood of future success. (a subtype of **criterion validity**)

> **Ex**
>
> If an assessment is used to select high school students for admission into a college or university (SAT in the US), the expectation is that the SAT is able to predict to some extent the test-takers' readiness for and subsequent performance in college or university courses.

47 Proficiency test***

The purpose of the test is to test <u>global competence</u> in a language. <u>It tests overall ability regardless of any training they previously had in the language.</u> Proficiency tests have traditionally consisted of the *standardized multiple-choices item on grammar, vocabulary, reading comprehension, and listening comprehension.* One of the standardized proficiency tests is TOEFL.

48 Rational deletion (in Cloze test)***

choosing deletions <u>according to the grammatical or discourse functions</u> of the words

49 Reliability***

A test is <u>consistent and dependable.</u> If you give the same test to the same student or matched students on two different occasions, the test should yield similar results.

50 Rubrics***

<u>specified categories</u>, which break down a skill <u>into several components,</u> for scoring or evaluating language performance

51　Self- and peer- assessment***

Students are usually frank and honest in their assessment of their own performance and that of their peers. Although one of the greatest drawbacks to self-assessment is the inevitable subjectivity of the process, you can maximize the beneficial washback of self-assessments by showing students the advantage of honest, objective opinions. Peer assessment supports students and teachers alike, reduces workload, and increases engagement and understanding. Student insights and observations are valued. They are important because they help the students reflect on and understand the process of their own learning.

52　Student-related reliability***

The most common learner-related issue in reliability is caused by temporary illness, fatigue, a "bad day," anxiety, and other physical or psychological factors, which may make an "observed" score deviate from one's "true" score.

09

53　Subjective test (e.g., extended-response questions, essays)***

This is a form of questioning that may have more than one correct answer. (or more than one way of expressing the correct answer)

54　Summative assessment / test***

evaluation of the final products, performances, and usually end-of-course or end-of-unit overall evaluation
In an educational setting, THIS is typically used to assign students a course grade. These types of assessments are generally evaluative.
It serves the purpose of "summing up" what students can perform. Placement tests, final exams, and end-of-unit tests are typical of this category.

55 Test [Ⓔ]

a method (usually an instrument) that <u>systematically measures</u> a person's ability or knowledge in a given domain
a subset of assessment

56 Test reliability^{★★☆}

A test might be unreliable if, for example, <u>items are not well calibrated for difficulty, poorly designed, or unfairly distributed</u>. Measures of test reliability are rarely the province of classroom-based assessment, but rather of statistical psychometric research.

57 Validity^{★★☆}

the extent to which <u>inferences made from assessment results are appropriate, meaningful, and useful</u> in terms of the purpose of the assessment

58 Washback^{★★★}

the effects, <u>both beneficial and detrimental,</u> of an assessment on teaching and learning prior to and after the assessment itself

※ **Read the following descriptions and fill in the blanks.**

01 _____ **test**

The purpose of THIS is to determine whether course objectives have been met with skills acquired by the end of a period of instruction. THIS should be limited to particular material addressed in a curriculum within a particular time frame. THIS belongs to summative because they are administered at the end of a unit/ term of study. It analyzes the extent to which students have acquired language that has already been taught.

02 _____ **assessment (e.g. portfolios, journals, self- and peer -assessment)**

THIS is a method of evaluation that measures a student's level of proficiency in a subject as opposed to the student's level of knowledge. The overall goal of THIS is to allow students to demonstrate their knowledge and execute tasks.

03 _____ _____ **method**

For classroom instruction, holistic scoring provides little washback into the writer's / speaker's further stages of learning. Classroom evaluation of learning is best served through THIS, in which as many as major elements of writing / speaking are scored, thus enabling learners to capture their weaknesses and strengths.

04 _____ **assessment**

THIS is a form of assessment in which students are asked to perform real-world tasks that demonstrate meaningful application of essential knowledge and skills. THIS engages students in applying knowledge and skills in the same way they are used in the "real world" outside school. It is performance-based assessment that requires a student to go beyond basic recall and demonstrate significant, worthwhile knowledge and understanding through a product, performance or exhibition. The assessment comprises an authentic task such as *participating in politically oriented debates, writing for the school newspaper, conduct a research group meeting or perform scientific research.*

05 _____ (of a test)

the degree of correspondence of the characteristics of a given language test task to the features of a target language task

Essentially, when you make a claim for THIS in a test task, you are saying that this task is likely to be enacted in the "real world."

06 _____ test

In written language, a sentence with a word left out should have enough context that a reader can close that gap with a calculated guess, using linguistic expectancies (formal schemata), back-ground experience (content schemata), and some strategic competence.

07 _____ validity

The extent of the agreement between two measures or assessments taken at the same time. It compares a new assessment with one that has already been tested and proven to be valid. (a subtype of **criterion validity**)

A test has THIS if its results are supported by other concurrent performance.

> **Ex** If the new test results correlate with the existing validated measure, THIS can be established.

08 _____ **validity**

the extent to which a test actually taps into the theoretical construct that it proposes to assess

"Proficiency" and "communicative competence" are a linguistic construct. ("Does this test actually tap into the theoretical construct as it has been defined?")

09 _____ **validity**

If a test actually samples the subject matter about which conclusions are to be drawn, and if it requires the test-taker to perform the behavior that is being measured, it can claim *content-related* *evidence* of validity.

09

10 _____ **validity**

the extent to which the "THIS" of the test has actually been reached

In the case of teacher-made classroom assessments, *THIS-related evidence* is best demonstrated through a comparison of results of an assessment with results of some other measure of the same THIS. (**Ex** concurrent validity, predictive validity)

11 _____ **test**

This occurs when candidates are measured against defined (and objective) criteria. It is designed to give test-takers feedback on specific course or lesson objectives.

12 _____ **(related to Cloze test)**

The second half (according to the number of letters) of every other word is obliterated, and the test-taker must restore each word.

13 _____ **test**

an assessment instrument designed to analyze a test-taker's strengths and weaknesses in terms of grammar, pronunciation, fluency, discourse, or other targeted linguistic features
The test offers a checklist of features for the teacher to use in discovering difficulties. This test will typically offer more detailed sub-categorized information on the learner.

14 _____ **test**

Testing involves the test-taker in actually performing the target task.

15 _____ _____ **testing (e.g., multiple-choice, grammar item)**

assessment on the assumption that language could be broken down into its component parts and those parts adequately tested
Language is segmented into many small linguistic points and the four language skills of listening, speaking, reading and writing. Test questions are designed to test these skills and linguistic points.

16 _____ **(efficiency) analysis**

Analyzing incorrect alternatives is useful in determining the relative usefulness of the decoys in each item.

17 _____ **validity**

the extent to which a test, on the "THIS" of it, appears from the learner's perspective to test what it is designed to test

18 _____ **deletion (in Cloze test)**

Typically every seventh word (plus or minus two) is deleted.

19 _____ **assessment**

deliberate, planned assessment using scoring and grading criteria and usually with conventionalized feedback
systematic, planned sampling techniques to assess students' achievement
It has conventionalized feedback.

> **Ex** exercises, or procedures specifically designed to tap into skills and knowledge

20 _____ **assessment / test**

ongoing informal evaluation serving the purpose of facilitating improvement in a student's performance
In an educational setting, THIS might be a teacher (or peer) or the learner providing feedback on a student's work, and would not necessarily be used for grading purposes. THIS is diagnostic.
It helps students to "check" progress, to discern areas that need improvement, and to give them some future goals to pursue.

21 _____ _____ **(standardized tests)**

instruments used to make crucial decisions about one's future path (**Ex** college entrance, employment, certification)

22 _____ _____ **method**

Uses a rubric for scoring (spoken / written) production holistically. Each point on a holistic scale is given a <u>systematic set of descriptors</u>, and the reader-evaluator matches <u>an overall impression with the descriptors</u> to arrive at <u>a score</u>.

23 _____ **test**

In THIS test, learners are <u>not performing the task</u> itself but rather a task <u>that is related</u> in some way.

24 _____ **assessment**

incidental, unplanned evaluation usually <u>embedded in classroom tasks</u>, and usually designed to elicit improved performance. (see also **formal assessment**) Usually, it has no specific scoring or grading formats.
(Ex teacher's <u>incidental, unplanned comments and responses</u> like Nice job! Did you say can or can't? You 'go' to the movies yesterday? or <u>a marginal comment on a paper</u>)

25 _____ **testing (e.g., interviews, cloze test)**

THIS attempts to assess a learner's capacity to <u>use many bits all at the same time</u>, and possibly while exercising several presumed components of a grammatical system, and perhaps more than <u>one of the traditional skills or aspects of skills</u>.

26 _____ _____ **(reliability)**

THIS looks at each item in a test that measures the same content. It assesses <u>the correlation between multiple items in a test</u> that are intended to measure the same construct. THIS is a type of reliability used to determine the validity of similar items on a test. All questions on a test proposed to measure certain content should produce similar and consistent results. Researchers use THIS to ensure that each item on a test is related to the topic they are researching. Ensuring items on a test are relevant to the study and measuring the same construct ensures that the test is valid. As a result, other researchers can depend on the results. Not having consistent reliability in a study renders the test results invalid. A test without THIS reliability could create questionable results that may not create usable data. The three measures are *Cronbach's Alpha, split-half test, and Kuder-Richardson test.* As one example, Cronbach's Alpha has a range of 0-1. The closer to 1, the more reliable the assessment. The scale determines how much agreement each item in a test has. The more agreement, the more the question are aligned or alike. The scale is as follows:

* **0.00-0.69** = Poor alignment
* **0.70-0.79** = Fair alignment
* **0.80-0.89** = Good alignment
* **0.90-0.99** = Excellent/strong alignment

09

27 _____ **reliability**

Human error, subjectivity, and bias may enter into the scoring process. THIS occurs when two or more scorers yield inconsistent scores of the same test, possibly for lack of attention to scoring criteria, inexperience, inattention, or even preconceived biases. In the story above about the placement test, the initial scoring plan for the dictations was found to be unreliable- that is, the two scorers were not applying the same standards.

28 _____ **reliability**

the degree of agreement among repeated administrations of a diagnostic test performed by a single rater

29 _____ _____

the extent to which <u>an item differentiates between high-and low-ability test-takers</u>. If a test is given to a large group of people, the discriminating power of an item can be measured by <u>comparing the number of people with high test scores who answered that item correctly with the number of people with low scores who answered the same item correctly</u>. If a particular item is doing a good job of discriminating between those who score high and those who score low, more people in the top-scoring group will have answered the item correctly. ($-1 < $ ID $ < 1$) Items with a ID of ≥ 0.35 were considered excellent, those between $0.2 - 0.34$ were considered acceptable and those < 0.2 were considered poor.

30 _____ _____ **(=item difficulty)**

This is the extent to which an item is easy or difficult for the proposed group of test-takers.
* **P** = The number of correct responses divided by the number of total test takers
* **0** = difficult item, **1** = easy item

31 _____ **test**

instrument in which each <u>test-taker's score is interpreted in relation to</u> a mean, median, standard deviation, and/or <u>percentile rank</u>

32 _____ **test (e.g., multiple-choice, true or false answers, matching questions)**

This is a form of questioning that has <u>a single correct answer.</u>

33 _____ _____ (_____ _____)

An approach to educational assessment that requires students to <u>directly demonstrate</u> what they know and are able to do through <u>open-ended tasks</u> such as *constructing an answer, producing a project, or performing an activity.* It is a form of testing that requires students to perform a task rather than select an answer from a ready-made list. For example, a student may be asked to generate scientific hypothesis, solve mathematics problems, converse in foreign language. The modes include: *open-ended or extended response exercise; extended tasks; and portfolios, teacher observation, oral presentations, hands-on problems, real world simulation* and *other authentic tasks.* Advocates said that THIS may be a more valued indicator of what students know and what he is able to do (knowledge & abilities) promotes active learning and curricula-based testing.

34 _____ **test**

The purpose of THIS is to <u>place a student into a particular level</u> or section of a language curriculum or school. It usually includes <u>a sampling of the material to be covered in the various courses in a curriculum.</u> That is, it has content validity. A student's performance on the test should indicate the point at which the student will find material neither too easy nor too difficult.

35 _____

<u>a purposeful collection of students' work</u> that demonstrates ... their efforts, progress, and achievements in given areas. This includes materials such as... *essays and compositions in draft and final forms; reports, project outlines; artwork, photos, newspaper or magazine clippings; audio and/or video recordings of presentations, demonstrations, etc.; self and peer-assessments.* The term 'THIS' is used to describe an instrument for recording progress (process) and ability (product) in the target language. This could be as simple as a pen and paper notebook, or as extensive as a computer-based record-keeping

tool. THIS can be used to support learning by encouraging learners to reflect on the language learning process, to record experiences in using the language, and get motivation based on their achievement recorded. THIS is often used as learning or teaching aids in learner-centered approaches to encourage critical reflection and to give some degree of control over the learning process to the language learner.

36 _____

the extent to which an instrument is within desirable financial limitations, time constraints, and ease of administration, scoring, and interpretation

A prohibitively expensive test is impractical. A test of language proficiency that takes a student five hours to complete is impractical – it consumes more time (and money) than necessary to accomplish its objective.

37 _____ **validity**

the capacity of an assessment to predict future performance

THIS of an assessment becomes important in the case of placement tests, admissions assessment batteries, language aptitude tests, and the like. The assessment criterion in such cases is not to measure concurrent ability but to assess (and predict) a test-taker's likelihood of future success. (a subtype of **criterion validity**)

If an assessment is used to select high school students for admission into a college or university (SAT in the US), the expectation is that the SAT is able to predict to some extent the test-takers' readiness for and subsequent performance in college or university courses.

38 _____ **test**

The purpose of THIS is to test <u>global competence</u> in a language. It tests overall ability regardless of any training they previously had in the language. THIS has traditionally consisted of the *standardized multiple-choices item on grammar, vocabulary, reading comprehension, and listening comprehension.* One of the standardized examples is TOEFL.

39 _____ _____ **(in Cloze test)**

choosing deletions <u>according to the grammatical or discourse functions</u> of the words

40 _____

A test is <u>consistent and dependable</u>. If you give the same test to the same student or matched students on two different occasions, the test should yield similar results.

41 _____

<u>specified categories</u>, which break down a skill <u>into several components</u>, for scoring or evaluating language performance

42 _____ _____ _____ **assessment**

Students are usually frank and honest in their assessment of their own performance and that of their peers. Although one of the greatest drawbacks to self-assessment is the inevitable subjectivity of the process, you can maximize the beneficial washback of self-assessments by showing students the advantage of honest, objective opinions. Peer assessment supports students and teachers alike, reduces workload, and increases engagement and understanding. Student insights and observations are valued. They are important because they help the students reflect on and understand the process of their own learning.

43 _____ **reliability**

The most common learner-related issue in reliability is caused by temporary illness, fatigue, a "bad day," anxiety, and other physical or psychological factors, which may make an "observed" score deviate from one's "true" score.

44 _____ **test (e.g., extended-response questions, essays)**

This is a form of questioning that may have more than one correct answer. (or more than one way of expressing the correct answer)

45 _____ **assessment / test**

evaluation of the final products, performances, and usually end-of-course or end-of-unit overall evaluation
In an educational setting, THIS is typically used to assign students a course grade. These types of assessments are generally evaluative.
It serves the purpose of "summing up" what students can perform. Placement tests, final exams, and end-of-unit tests are typical of this category.

46 _____

the extent to which inferences made from assessment results are appropriate, meaningful, and useful in terms of the purpose of the assessment

47 _____

the effects, both beneficial and detrimental, of an assessment on teaching and learning prior to and after the assessment itself

Answers

01 Achievement

02 Alternative

03 Analytic scoring

04 Authentic

05 Authenticity

06 Cloze

07 Concurrent

08 Construct

09 Content

10 Criterion

11 Criterion-referenced

12 C-test

13 Diagnostic

14 Direct

15 Discrete point

16 Distractor

17 Face

18 Fixed-ratio

19 Formal

20 Formative

21 High stakes

22 Holistic scoring

23 Indirect

24 Informal

25 Integrative

26 Internal consistency

27 Inter-rater

28 Intra-rater

29 Item discrimination

30 Item facility

31 Norm-referenced

32 Objective

33 Performance assessment / Performance-based assessment

34 Placement

35 Portfolio(s)

36 Practicality

37 Predictive

38 Proficiency

39 Rational deletion

40 Reliability

41 Rubrics

42 Self- and peer-

43 Student-related

44 Subjective

45 Summative

46 Validity

47 Washback

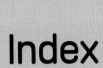

Index

Index

A

Abductive approach	227
Acculturation	098
Accultutation model	098
Accuracy (in terms of speaking skills)	184
Accuracy	227
Achievement test	268
Acquisition	014
Acquisition-learning hypothesis	014
Action research	098
Activity	099
Adaptive Control of Thought (ACT) model (by John Anderson)	014
Additive bilingualism	015
Adjunct model (of content-based language teaching)	099
Adjacency pair (in conversation analysis)	184
Advance organizer	162
Affective domain	060
Affective factors	060
Affective filter (by Stephan Krashen)	060
Affective filter hypothesis	015
Affective strategy(ies)	060
Agency	060
Alternative assessment (e.g. portfolios, journals, self- and peer-assessment)	268
Ambiguity intolerance	061
Ambiguity tolerance (tolerance of ambiguity)	061
Amotivation	061
Analytic learning style	061
Analytic scoring method	268
Analyzed language	015
Anomie	015
	099
Anxiety	062
Approach	099

Appropriateness	228
Appropriate word scoring (acceptable word method)(in Cloze test)	268
Artifact(s)	099
Artifact study	099
Assessment	269
Attention	228
Attention getting	185
Audiolingual Method (ALM)	100
Audiolingualism	016
Audio-motor unit	100
Auditory learning style	062
Authentic assessment	269
Authentic language	162
Authenticity (of a test)	269
Automatic processes (=processing) / Automaticity	016
Autonomy	100
Avoidance	062
Awareness	016
	228
Awareness-raising	016
	228

B

Backsliding	016
Basal readers (Basal approach, Bottom-up)	162
Basic Interpersonal Communication Skills (BICS)	062
Behaviorism	017
Biligualism	017
Blended learning	101
Bottom-up (data-driven) processing	163
Bottom-up processing	147
Brainstorming	209

Breadth of knowledge 228

C

Checklist 209
Chunk / Chunking (clustering) 147
185
Classroom-based assessment 101
270
Classroom language 101
Classroom management 101
Cloze test 270
Cognition 017
Cognitive strategies 063
Cognitive style 063
Coherence 017
Cohesion 018
Collaboration 063
Collocation 229
Communication Strategies 063
(DÖrnyel, 1995)
Communicative 101
Communicative competence 102
(Canal and Swain, 1983)
Communicative competence 102
(Littlewood, 2011)
Communicative Language Teaching 018
(CLT)
Communicative language test 270
Communicative task 103
① information-gap activity
② opinion-gap activity
③ reasoning-gap activity
Communities of Practice (CoP) 103
Community Language Learning (CLL) 104
Compensatory strategies 063
(communication strategies)
① avoidance
② circumlocution

③ approximation
④ word coinage
⑤ prefabricated patterns
⑥ code-switching
⑦ appeal to authority
⑧ literal translation
⑨ keeping the floor
⑩ foreignizing
⑪ nonlinguistic signals
Competence 019
Complexity 229
Composing 209
Compound bilingualism 019
Comprehensible input 019
Comprehensible output hypothesis 019
Comprehension 019
Computer-adaptive Testing (CAT) 104
(=tailored testing)
Computer-assisted Language 104
Learning (CALL)
Computer-mediated Communication 104
(CMC)
Concordance 104
230
Concordancer 230
Concordancing 105
230
Concurrent validity 270
Conferencing 209
Connotation 230
Conscious learning 020
Consciousness-raising task (CR task) 231
Construct validity 271
Content schemata 163
Content validity 271
Content-based instruction (CBI) / 105
Content-based Language Teaching (CBLT)
① Immersion model
② Sheltered model
③ Adjunct model

www.pmg.co.kr

④ Theme-based instruction
cf. subject-integrated class

Contextual knowledge	147
	163
Contrastive alanysis	064
Contrastive Analysis Hypothesis (CAH)	020
Contrastive rhetoric	210
Controlled processes / processing	020
Controlled writing	210
Conversation Analysis (CA)	020
Conversational gambits	185
Conversational interactions	021
Cooperative learning	106
Coordinate bilingualism	021
Corpora	231
Corpus linguistics	106
	231
Corpus-based teaching	107
Covert error(s)	064
Criterion validity	271
Criterion-referenced test	271
Critical language assessment	272
Critical period hypothesis	021
Cross-linguistic Influence (CLI)	021
C-test (related to cloze test)	272
Culture assimilator	107
Culture capsule	107
Culture island	107
Culture shock	108
Culture stress	108
Curriculum	108

Deductive approach	232
Deductive reasoning	232
Demotivation	065
Depth of knowledge	232
Diagnostic test	271
Dialogue	148
Dialogue journal(s)	210
Dictocomp / Dicto-composition	210
Dictogloss	148
	232
Difficulty	065
Digital literacy	108
Dimensions of grammar	232
Direct method	109
Direct test	272
Directive (approaches to teaching)	109
Discourse	186
	211
Discourse markers	163
Discourse analysis	022
Discourse competence (one of communicative competence)	186
Discourse Completion Task (DCT)	186
Discovery learning	109
Discrete point testing (e.g. multiple-choice, grammar item)	272
Display question(s)	022
Display writing	211
Distractor (efficiency) analysis	273
Drill	022
Drill(s)	233

D

Debilitative anxiety	065
Declarative knowledge	021
	231

E

Elaboration	109
Electronic portfolio (e-portfolio)	273
Ellication	022

Ellipsis (related to cohesion)	023	Field Independence (FI)	067
Emergent stage	065	Field sensitivity	068
Emotional intelligence (EQ, Emotional	065	Fixed-ratio deletion (in Cloze test)	274
Quotient)		Flipped learning	110
Empathy	066	Fluency	187
English as a Foreign Language (EFL)	023	Focus on Form (FonF)	234
English as a Second Language (ESL)	023	Focus on Forms (FonFs)	234
English as an International Language	023	Focus on meaning	234
(EIL)		Form (of language)	234
English only (debate)	109	Formal assessment	274
Equilibration	066	Formal schemata	165
Error analysis	024	Formality	186
Error Correction Code (ECC)	211		211
Errors of addition, omission, substitution,	066	Formative assessment / test	274
and permutation		Form-focused Instruction (FFI)	235
Exact word method (in Cloze test)	273	Fossilization	025
Experiential learning	110	Freewriting	212
Explicit instruction	233	Frequency	235
Explicit knowledge	024	Functional syllabus	111
	233		
Explicit (treatment of form)	234		
Exploitability (for choosing reading texts)	164		
Extensive listening (listening for pleasure)	148	**G**	
Extensive reading	165	Garden path	235
Extent	066	Genre	212
Extra-class work	110	Genre-based approach / writing	212
Extrinsic motivation	067	Global error(s)	068
Extroversion	067		235
Eye contact	110	Global self-esteem	068
		Goal	111
		Graded reader(s)	165
		Grammar consciousness raising	025
F		Grammaring	236
Face validity	273	Grammar translation method	111
Facilitation	024	Grammatical competence	187
Facilitative anxiety	067	(or linguistic competence, one of	
Feedback type	024	communicative comperence	
Field Dependence (FD)	067	Grammaticality	236

Grammaticalization	236
Graphic Organizers (GO)	165
Group dynamics	111
Group work	111
Guessing	166
Guided writing	212

H

Halliday's seven functions of language	025
(Developmetal functions of language)	
Haptics	187
Hierarchy of difficulty	026
High Input Generators (HIGs)	068
High stakes (standardized tests)	274
Holistic scoring method	275
Hypercorrection	068
	236

I

Identity	069
Idiosyncratic dialect	026
Illocutionary competence	187
Illocutionary force	187
Immersion	112
Implicit instruction	237
Implicit knowledge	026
	237
Implicit learning	237
Implicit (treatment of form)	237
Impulsivity (impulsive style)	069
Incidental learning	238
Indicator (Varonis and Gass's (1985)	026
model of negotiation)	
Indirect test	275
Induced error(s)	069
Inductive approach	238

Inductive reasoning	238
Inferencing	166
Inferential listening	149
Informal assessment	275
Information exchange	188
Information gap activity	188
Information transfer	149
Inhibition	069
Inner circle	112
Input	027
Input enhancement	238
Input flooding	239
Input hypothesis	026
Input modification	112
Input processing	239
Instrumental orientation	070
Intake	027
Intergrated approach / skills	027
Integrative orientation	070
Integrative testing (e.g. interviews,	275
cloze test)	
Intelligibility	188
Intensive listening (listening for a purpose)	149
Intensive reading	166
Intentional learning	239
Interaction hypothesis	028
Interactional competence	070
Interactive processing	167
Intercultural competence	070
Intercultural rhetoric	213
Interface hypothesis	028
Interference	029
Interlanguage (4 developmental stages:	070
pre-systematic stage, emergent stage,	
systematic stage, stabilization stage)	
Interlingual transfer	029
	071
Internal consistency (reliability)	276
Internalization	029
Interpersonal dialogue	149

Inter-rater reliability	276
Intralingual transfer	029
	071
Intra-rater reliability	276
Intrinsic motivation	071
Introversion	071
Item difficulty	277
Item discrimination	277
Item facility (=Item difficulty)	277

J

Jigsaw	189
Jigsaw listening	150
Journals	277

K

Keyword method / technique	240
Kinesics	112
Kinesthetics	112
Kinesthetic learning style	072

L

Language Acquisition Device (LAD)	029
Language anxiety	072
Language ego	072
Language competence (Bachman, 1990)	113
Language Experience Approach (LEA, 1967) (Top-down)	167
Learnability	072
Learner-centered instruction	113
Learner language	073
Learning strategies	073
Learning style	073

Left-brain dominance	073
Lexical approach	113
	240
Lexical cohesion (related to cohesion)	030
Lexico-grammatical approach	114
	240
Linguistic approach (Bottom-up)	167
Listening for details	150
Listening for gist	150
Literature-based approach (Top-down)	168
Local error(s)	073
	241
Low Input Generators (LIGs)	073

M

Macroskills	114
Markedness differential hypothsis (=Markedness theory)	030
Meaningful drill(s)	241
Meaningful learning	030
Meaningful minimal pairs	189
Mechanical drill(s)	241
Metacognitive strategy(ies)	074
Metalanguage	114
Metalinguistic explanation	189
Microskills	114
Minimal pairs	189
Mobile-assisted Language Learning (MALL)	114
Modified input	031
	115
Modified interaction	031
Modified output	032
Monitor hypothesis	032
Monitoring	150
Monologue	151

Motivation	032
	074
Multimodal communication	115
Multiple intelligence	033

N

Native English-speaking Teachers (NESTs)	115
Native informant	115
Natural approach	116
Natural order hypothesis	033
Needs analysis / Needs assessment	116
Negative evidence	033
Negative transfer	033
Negotiation of form	034
Negotiation of meaning (=meaning-negotiation strategies)	034
Negotiation of meaning	190
① comprehension check	
② clarification request	
③ confirmation check	
Nondirective (approach to teaching)	117
Nonnative English-speaking Teachers (NNESTs)	117
Norm-referenced test	278
Noticing hypothesis	034
Noticing the gap	034
Notional-functional syllabus (=functional syllabus)	117

O

Objective	117
Objective needs	117
Objective test (e.g. multiple-choice, true or false answers, matching questions)	278
Oculesics	118

Olfactory	118
Online planning (on-line planning, within-task planning)	118
Optimal distance model	118
Oral dialogue journals	190
Orientation	074
Outer circle	118
Output	035
Overgeneralization	035
Overt error(s)	074

P

Pacing	119
Pair work	119
Pedagogical task(s) (=pedagogic task(s))	119
Peer pressure	075
Peer-editing	213
Perceived social distance	119
Performance	036
Performance assessment	278
Perlocutionary force	190
Personalization	036
Phonics approach (Bottom-up)	168
Picture description task	191
Placement test	278
Portfolio(s)	279
Positive evidence	036
Positive transfer	036
Postsystematic stage	075
PPP: Presentation → Practice → Production	120
PPP (presentation, practice, production)	241
Practicality	279
Pragmalinguistics	037
Pragmatic competence	191
Predicting	151
Predictive validity	279
Prefabricated patterns	075

Presystematic (error) 075
Procative inhibition 075
Procedural knowledge 037
241
Procedure 120
Process 120
Processing instruction 242
Process-oriented approach 213
Process-oriented syllabus 120
Product 120
Productive knowledge 242
Product-oriented approach 213
Product-oriented syllabus 121
Proficiency 037
Proficiency test 280
Program 121
Project-based Learning (PBL) 121
Psychological distance 122
Psycholinguistics 038
Pushed output 038

R

Rational deletion (in Cloze test) 280
Rapport 076
Reaction to response (Varonis and 038
Gass's (1985) model of negotiation)
Readability (for choosing reading texts) 168
Real writing 213
Realia 122
Recast 038
Receptive knowledge 242
Reduced forms 151
Redundancy 152
Reference (related to cohesion) 039
Referential question(s) 039
Reflectivity (reflective style) 076
Register 191
Regulation 039

Rehearsal 040
192
Reliability 280
Repair 040
Repetition 040
Response (Varonis and Gass's (1985) 040
model of negotiation)
Restructuring 242
Retrocative Inhabition 076
Rhetorical formality (in writing) 214
Right-brain dominance 077
Risk taking 077
Role-play(s) 192
Role(s) 192
Rote learning (≒Rote memorizing) 041
Rubrics 280

S

Salience 243
Scaffolding 041
Scanning 152
168
Schema theory 169
Schemata 169
Schematic knowledge (cf. schemata) 041
Second identity 077
Second Language Acquisition (SLA) 041
Segmentals (teaching pronounciation) 192
Self-actualization 077
Self- and peer- assessment 281
Self-correction 077
Self-determination 077
Self-efficacy 078
Self-esteem 078
Self-regulation 041
078
Self-writing 214
Semantic mapping / Clustering 169

Sentence combining	214	Student-related reliability	281
Series method	122	Styles	080
Sheltered model (sheltered-language	122	Styles (in speech discourse)	195
instruction)		Subject-integrated class	126
Shifting (of a topic)	193	Subjective needs	126
Silent period	042	Subjective test (e.g. extended-response	281
Simplification	122	questions, essays)	
Simulation(s)	193	Substitution (related to cohesion)	042
Situation analysis	123	Subtractive bilingualism	042
Situation self-esteem	078	Suitability of content (for choosing	170
Skimming	169	reading texts)	
Social distance	123	Summative assessment / test	281
Socioaffective strategies	078	Suprasegmentals (teaching pronounciation)	195
Sociocultural awareness	123	Sustained Deep Learning (SDL)	126
Sociocultural Theory (SCT)	042	Syllabus	127
Sociocultural-interactive (S-I) strategy	079	Systematicity	081
Sociolinguistic competence	079		
(≒sociocultural competence)			
Sociolinguistic competence (one of	193		
communicative competence)			
Sociopragmatics	124	Tactics	127
Speech acts	124	Target task(s)	127
Speech styles	193	Task self-esteem	081
Spiral learning	125	Task type (Richard, 2001)	195
SQ3R	170	① jigsaw	
Stabilization	079	② information-gap	
State anxiety	079	③ problem-solving	
Storytelling	194	④ decision-making	
Strategic competence	079	⑤ opinion exchange	
Strategic competence (one of	194	Task-based Language Teaching (TBLT)	127
communicative competence)		Teachability hypothesis	128
Strategic self-regulation (S2R)	080		245
Strategies-based Instruction (SBI)	125	Teacher-centered instruction	128
Strategy	080	Teacher's roles	129
Structural syllabus	125	Teaching styles	128
Structured input	243	Technique(s)	129
Structured input activities	243	Terminal objective	129
Structured output	244	Termination (of a topic)	197

Test 282
Test reliability 282
Textbook adaptation 129
Theme-based instruction 130
Think-aloud strategy / technique 130
Tolerance of ambiguity 081
Top-down (concept-driven) processing 170
Top-down processing 152
Topic clarification 197
Topic development 197
Topic nomination 197
Total Physical Response (TPR) 130
Trait anxiety 081
Transactional dialogue 152
Transfer 043
Translanguaging 131
Trigger (Varonis and Gass's (1985) 043
model of negotiation)
Turn-taking 043
197

U

U-shaped acquisition / development / 043
learning
Unanalyzed language 044
Uncertainty avoidance 131
Universal Grammar (UG) 044
Uptake 044

V

Validity 282
Variation (=variability) 081
Visual, auditory, tactile, knesthetic 082
learning styles
Vocabulary analysis (=word analysis) 245

W

Washback 282
Willingness To Communicate (WTC) 082
Whole language education 045
Word family(ies) 245
Word formation 246
Word-learning strategies 246
Word map 246
Working memory 082
World Englishes 131

Z

Zone of Proximal Development (ZPD) 045

KEYTERM MASTER

for EFL teachers

초판인쇄 | 2024. 6. 13. **초판발행** | 2024. 6. 20.

편저자 | 송은우 **발행인** | 박 용 **발행처** | (주)박문각출판

등록 | 2015년 4월 29일 제2019-000137호

주소 | 06654 서울시 서초구 효령로 283 서경B/D 4층

팩스 | (02)584-2927

전화 | 교재 주문·내용 문의 (02)6466-7202

저자와의
협의하에
인지생략

이 책의 무단 전재 또는 복제 행위는 저작권법 제136조에 의거, 5년 이하의 징역 또는
5,000만 원 이하의 벌금에 처하거나 이를 병과할 수 있습니다.

정가 20,000원   ISBN 979-11-7262-035-6